D1104564

Rethinking Transportation

2020-2030

*The Disruption of Transportation and
the Collapse of the Internal-Combustion
Vehicle and Oil Industries*

James Arbib & Tony Seba

Printed in the United States of America
First Edition

ISBN 978-0-9994016-0-6
For information about quantity discounts or about permission to reproduce selections
from this book, Email: info@rethinkx.com
www.rethinkX.com

Cover Art © 2017 by RethinkX.
Many of the product names referred to herein are trademarks or registered trademarks
of their respective owners.

Library of Congress Cataloging-in-Publication Data

Arbib, James and Seba, Tony
Rethinking Transportation 2020-2030: The Disruption of Transportation
and the Collapse of the Internal-Combustion Vehicle and Oil Industries
-1st ed.

Includes bibliographical references and index.
ISBN 978-0-9994016-0-6

» Contents

The **Rethink**X Project

RethinkX is an independent think tank that analyzes and forecasts the speed and scale of technology-driven disruption and its implications across society. We produce compelling, impartial data-driven analyses that identify pivotal choices to be made by investors, businesses, policymakers and civic leaders.

Rethinking Transportation is the first in a series that analyzes the impacts of technology-driven disruption, sector by sector, across the economy. We aim to produce analyses that reflect the reality of fast-paced technology-adoption S-curves. Mainstream analysts have produced linear and incremental forecasts that have consistently underplayed the speed and extent of technological disruptions, as in, for example, solar PV and mobile phone adoption forecasts. By relying on these mainstream forecasts, policymakers, investors and businesses risk locking in sub-optimal pathways.

RethinkX's follow-on analyses will consider the cascading and interdependent effects of this disruption within and across sectors. Our aim is to facilitate a global conversation about the threats and opportunities of technology-driven disruption and to focus attention on choices that can help lead to a more equitable, healthy, resilient and stable society.

We invite you to join our community of thought leaders and experts to better inform this conversation.

To learn more, please visit www.rethinkx.com.

Follow us at **/rethink_x**

 /JoinRethinkX

 /company/rethinkx

RethinkTransportation

» Preface

The analysis in this report is based on detailed evaluation of data on the market, consumer and regulatory dynamics that work together to drive disruption. We present an economic analysis based on existing technologies that have well-known cost curves and on existing business-model innovations. We extrapolate data where we have credible knowledge that these cost curves will continue in the near future. The disruptions we highlight might happen more quickly due to the acceleration of the cost curves (such as has been happening in lithium-ion batteries, for example) or because of step changes in these technologies (such as has been happening in solid-state batteries and artificial-intelligence processing units). New business-model innovations may also accelerate disruption.

Our findings and their implications are based on following the data and applying our knowledge of finance, economics, technology adoption and human behavior. Our findings show the speed, scale and implications of the disruptions to be expected in a rational context. Scenarios can only be considered in terms of probabilities. We think the scenarios we lay out to be far more probable than others currently forecast. In fact, we consider these disruptions to be inevitable. Ultimately, individual consumers, businesses, investors and policymakers will make the decisions that dictate how these disruptions unfold. We provide insights that anticipate disruption. Hopefully we can all make better decisions to benefit society based on the evidence that we present.

» Disclaimer

Any findings, predictions, inferences, implications, judgments, beliefs, opinions, recommendations, suggestions and similar matters in this Report are statements of opinion by the authors, and are not statements of fact. You should treat them as such and come to your own conclusions based upon your own research. The content of this Report does not constitute advice of any kind and you should not take any action or refrain from taking any action in reliance upon this Report or the contents thereof.

This Report includes possible scenarios selected by the authors. The scenarios are not designed to be comprehensive or necessarily representative of all situations. Any scenario or statement in this Report is based upon certain assumptions and methodologies chosen by the authors. Other assumptions and/ or methodologies may exist which could lead to other results and/or opinions.

Neither the authors nor publisher of this Report, nor any of their respective affiliates, directors, officers, employees, partners, licensors, agents or representatives provide any financial or investment advice by virtue of publishing and/or distributing this Report and nothing in this Report should be construed as constituting financial or investment advice of any kind or nature. Neither the authors nor publisher of this Report, nor any of their respective affiliates, directors, officers, employees, partners, licensors, agents or representatives make any recommendation or representation regarding the advisability of purchasing, investing in or making any financial commitment with respect to any asset, property and/ or business and nothing in this Report should be construed as such. A decision to purchase, invest in or make any financial commitment with respect to any such asset, property and/or business should not be made in reliance on this Report or any information contained therein. The general information contained in this Report should not be acted upon without obtaining specific legal, tax and/or investment advice from a licensed professional.

Nothing in this Report constitutes an invitation or inducement to engage in investment activity for the purposes of section 21 of the Financial Services and Markets Act 2000.

No representations or warranties of any kind or nature, whether express or implied, are given in relation to this Report or the information contained therein. The authors and publishers of this Report disclaim, to the fullest extent permitted by applicable law, all representations and warranties of any kind or nature, whether express or implied, concerning this Report and the contents thereof.

To the fullest extent permitted by applicable law, the authors and publisher of this Report, and their respective affiliates, directors, officers, employees, partners, licensors, agents and representatives shall not be liable for:

- *any loss or damage suffered or incurred by you or any other person or entity as a result of any action that you or any other person or entity may take or refrain from taking as a result of this Report or any information contained therein;*
- *any dealings you may have with third parties as a result of this Report or any information contained therein; and*
- *any loss or damage which you or any other person or entity may suffer or incur as a result of or connected to your, or any other person's or entity's, use of this Report or any information contained therein.*

In this Disclaimer, references to this Report include any information provided by the authors or publisher, or any of their respective affiliates, directors, officers, employees, partners, licensors, agents or representatives which relates to this Report, including, without limitation, summaries, press releases, social media posts, interviews and articles concerning this Report.

RethinkTransportation

» With Thanks

This report would not have been possible without the support of a wide group of individuals and organizations who have provided insight and time. Many people contributed directly to this work and reviewed our assumptions and drafts of the report including:

Ryan Popple	*Tony Posawatz*	*Stephen Zoepf*
Mike Finnern	*Bart Riley*	*Deborah Gordon*
Bryan Hansel	*Ike Hong*	*David Livingston*
Simon Moores	*Kristina Church*	*Dan Sperling*
Casper Rawles	*Jonathan Short*	
Andrew Miller	*Alex Lightman*	
Rahul Sonnad	*Ed Maguire*	
Nick Warren	*Ian Welch*	

Many others have influenced the thinking and insight we have, particularly the huge number of people and organizations that Tony has spoken to over the past few years including many of the leading automotive, battery, oil and investment companies.

Our thanks in no way implies agreement with all (or any) of our assumptions and findings. Any mistakes are our own.

RethinkX Research and Co-Writing Team:

Irem Kok, Sani Ye Zou, Joshua Gordon and Bernard Mercer

RethinkX Research Operations and Management Team:

Uzair Niazi, Rosie Bosworth and Meena Raju

RethinkX Communications and Design Team:

Cater Communications - Morrow Cater, Sage Welch, Natalie Pawelski and Cristen Farley

» Executive Summary

We are on the cusp of one of the fastest, deepest, most consequential disruptions of transportation in history. By 2030, within 10 years of regulatory approval of autonomous vehicles (AVs), 95% of U.S. passenger miles traveled will be served by on-demand autonomous electric vehicles owned by fleets, not individuals, in a new business model we call "transport-as-a-service" (TaaS). The TaaS disruption will have enormous implications across the transportation and oil industries, decimating entire portions of their value chains, causing oil demand and prices to plummet, and destroying trillions of dollars in investor value — but also creating trillions of dollars in new business opportunities, consumer surplus and GDP growth.

The disruption will be driven by economics. Using TaaS, the average American family will save more than $5,600 per year in transportation costs, equivalent to a wage raise of 10%. This will keep an additional $1 trillion per year in Americans' pockets by 2030, potentially generating the largest infusion of consumer spending in history.

We have reached this conclusion through exhaustive analysis of data, market, consumer and regulatory dynamics, using well-established cost curves and assuming only existing technology. This report presents overwhelming evidence that mainstream analysis is missing, yet again, the speed, scope and impact of technology disruption. Unlike those analyses, which produce linear and incremental forecasts, our modeling incorporates systems dynamics, including feedback loops, network effects and market forces, that better reflect the reality of fast-paced technology-adoption S-curves. These systems dynamics, unleashed as adoption of TaaS begins, will create a virtuous cycle of decreasing costs and increasing quality of service and convenience, which will in turn drive further adoption along an exponential S-curve. Conversely, individual vehicle ownership, especially of internal combustion engine (ICE) vehicles, will enter a vicious cycle of increasing costs, decreasing convenience and diminishing quality of service.

» Summary of findings

- The approval of autonomous vehicles will unleash a highly competitive market-share grab among existing and new Pre-TaaS (ride-hailing) companies in expectation of the outsized rewards of trillions of dollars of market opportunities and network effects. Pre-TaaS platform providers like Uber, Lyft and Didi are already engaged, and others will join this high-speed race. Winners-take-all dynamics will force them to make large upfront investments to provide the highest possible level of service, ensuring supply matches demand in each geographic market they enter.

- In this intensely competitive environment, businesses will offer services at a price trending toward cost. As a result, their fleets will quickly transition from human-driven, internal combustion engine (ICE) vehicles to autonomous electric vehicles (A-EV) because of key cost factors, including ten times higher vehicle-utilization rates, 500,000-mile vehicle lifetimes (potentially improving to 1 million miles by 2030), and far lower maintenance, energy, finance and insurance costs.

- **As a result, transport-as-a-service (TaaS) will offer vastly lower-cost transport alternatives — four to ten times cheaper per mile than buying a new car and two to four times cheaper than operating an existing vehicle in 2021.**

- Other revenue sources from advertising, data monetization, entertainment and product sales will open a road to free transport in a TaaS Pool model, as private and public transportation begin to merge.

- Cost saving will also be the key factor in driving consumers to adopt TaaS.

- Adoption will start in cities and radiate outward to rural areas. Non-adopters will be largely restricted to the most rural areas, where cost and wait times are likely to be higher.

- High vehicle utilization (each car will be used at least 10 times more than individually owned cars) will mean that far fewer cars will be needed in the U.S. vehicle fleet, and therefore there will be no supply constraint to the speed and extent of TaaS adoption that we forecast.

Taken together, this analysis forecasts a very fast and extensive disruption: **TaaS will provide 95% of the passenger miles traveled within 10 years** of the widespread regulatory approval of AVs. By 2030, individually owned ICE vehicles will still represent 40% of the vehicles in the U.S. vehicle fleet, but they will provide just 5% of passenger miles.

Behavioral issues such as love of driving, fear of new technology or habit are generally believed to pose initial barriers to consumer uptake. However, Pre-TaaS companies such as Uber, Lyft and Didi have invested billions of dollars developing technologies and services to overcome these issues. In 2016, Pre-TaaS companies drove 500,000 passengers per day in New York City alone.[1] That was triple the number of passengers driven the previous year. The combination of TaaS's dramatically lower costs compared with car ownership and exposure to successful peer experience will drive more widespread usage of the service. Adopting TaaS requires no investment or lock-in. Consumers can try it with ease and increase usage as their comfort level increases. Even in suburban and rural areas, where wait times and cost might be slightly higher, adoption is likely to be more extensive than generally forecast because of the greater impact of cost savings on lower incomes. As with any technology disruption, adoption will grow along an exponential S-curve.[2]

The impacts of TaaS disruption are far reaching:

 Economic

‣ Savings on transportation costs will result in a permanent boost in annual disposable income for U.S. households, totaling $1 trillion by 2030. Consumer spending is by far the largest driver of the economy, comprising about 71% of total GDP and driving business and job growth throughout the economy.[3]

‣ Productivity gains as a result of reclaimed driving hours will boost GDP by an additional $1 trillion.

‣ As fewer cars travel more miles, the number of passenger vehicles on American roads will drop from 247 million to 44 million, opening up vast tracts of land for other, more productive uses. Nearly 100 million existing vehicles will be abandoned as they become economically unviable.

‣ Demand for new vehicles will plummet: 70% fewer passenger cars and trucks will be manufactured each year. This could result in total disruption of the car value chain, with car dealers, maintenance and insurance companies suffering almost complete destruction. Car manufacturers will have options to adapt, either as low-margin, high-volume assemblers of A-EVs, or by becoming TaaS providers. Both strategies will be characterized by high levels of competition, with new entrants from other industries. The value in the sector will be mainly in the vehicle operating systems, computing platforms and the TaaS platforms.

‣ The transportation value chain will deliver 6 trillion passenger miles in 2030 (an increase of 50% over 2021) at a quarter of the cost ($393 billion versus $1,481 billion).

‣ Oil demand will peak at 100 million barrels per day by 2020, dropping to 70 million barrels per day by 2030. That represents a drop of 30 million barrels in real terms and 40 million barrels below the Energy Information Administration's current "business as usual" case. This will have a catastrophic effect on the oil industry through price collapse (an equilibrium cost of $25.4 per barrel), disproportionately impacting different companies, countries, oil fields and infrastructure depending on their exposure to high-cost oil.

- The impact of the collapse of oil prices throughout the oil industry value chain will be felt as soon as 2021.

- In the U.S., an estimated 65% of shale oil and tight oil — which under a "business as usual" scenario could make up over 70% of the U.S. supply in 2030 — would no longer be commercially viable.

- Approximately 70% of the potential 2030 production of Bakken shale oil would be stranded under a 70 million barrels per day demand assumption.

- Infrastructure such as the Keystone XL and Dakota Access pipelines would be stranded, as well.

- Other areas facing volume collapse include offshore sites in the United Kingdom, Norway and Nigeria; Venezuelan heavy-crude fields; and the Canadian tar sands.

- Conventional energy and transportation industries will suffer substantial job loss. Policies will be needed to mitigate these adverse effects.

 Environmental

- The TaaS disruption will bring dramatic reductions or elimination of air pollution and greenhouse gases from the transport sector, and improved public health. The TaaS transport system will reduce energy demand by 80% and tailpipe emissions by over 90%. Assuming a concurrent disruption of the electricity infrastructure by solar and wind, we may see a largely carbon-free road transportation system by 2030.

Geopolitical

▸ The geopolitical importance of oil will vastly diminish. However, the speed and scale of the collapse in oil revenues may lead to the destabilization of oil-producing countries and regions with high dependence on oil "rents." This may create a new category of geopolitical risks. The geopolitics of lithium and other key mineral inputs to A-EVs are entirely different from oil politics. There will be no "Saudi Arabia of lithium." Lithium is a stock, while oil is a flow. Disruption in supply of the former does not impact service delivery. (See page 54 for further detail.)

Social

▸ TaaS will dramatically lower transportation costs; increase mobility and access to jobs, education and health care (especially for those restricted in today's model, like the elderly and disabled); create trillions of dollars in consumer surplus; and contribute to cleaner, safer and more walkable communities.

▸ We foresee a merging of public and private transportation and a pathway to free transportation in the TaaS Pool model (a subset of TaaS that entails sharing a ride with other people who are not in the passenger's family or social group — the equivalent of today's Uber Pool or Lyft Line). Corporations might sponsor vehicles or offer free transport to market goods or services to commuters (i.e. Starbucks Coffee on wheels[4]).

▸ The role of public transportation authorities (PTA) will change dramatically from owning and managing transportation assets, to managing TaaS providers to ensure equitable, universal access to low-cost transportation. Many municipalities will see free TaaS as a means to improve citizens' access to jobs, shopping, entertainment, education, health and other services within their communities.

» Conclusion

The aim of this research is to start a conversation and focus decision-makers' attention on the scale, speed and impact of the impending disruption in the transportation and oil sectors. Investors and policymakers will face choices in the near term that will have lasting impact. At critical junctures, their decisions will either help accelerate or slow down the transition to TaaS. Follow-on analysis by RethinkX will look more closely at each of these junctures and at the implications of potential decisions.

Many decisions will be driven by economic advantages (including return on investment, productivity gains, time savings, reduced infrastructure costs and GDP growth) as well as by social and environmental considerations (including fewer traffic deaths and injuries, increased access to mobility and emissions reductions). But other decisions may be influenced by incumbent industries seeking to delay or derail the disruption. Given the winners-take-all nature of the A-EV race, early movers to TaaS stand to gain outsized benefits.

Our main aim in starting this conversation is to provide an evidence-driven systems analysis that helps decision-makers who might otherwise rely purely on mainstream analysis. Decisions made based on the latter risk locking in investments and infrastructure that are sub-optimal — economically, socially and environmentally — and that will eventually lead to stranded assets. These sub-optimal decisions tend to make societies poorer by locking them into expensive, obsolete, uncompetitive assets, technologies and skill sets.

» The Seba Technology Disruption Framework™

RethinkX uses the Seba Technology Disruption Framework™ to help analyze and model the disruptions in this study. Developed by Tony Seba, this framework is the result of more than a dozen years of research and teaching on technology disruptions, business model innovation, finance and strategic marketing of high-tech products and innovations at Stanford Continuing Studies, and has been used to understand and anticipate disruptions in several industries. For a full description of the Seba Technology Disruption Framework, please see Appendix B.

Seba Technology Disruption Framework™

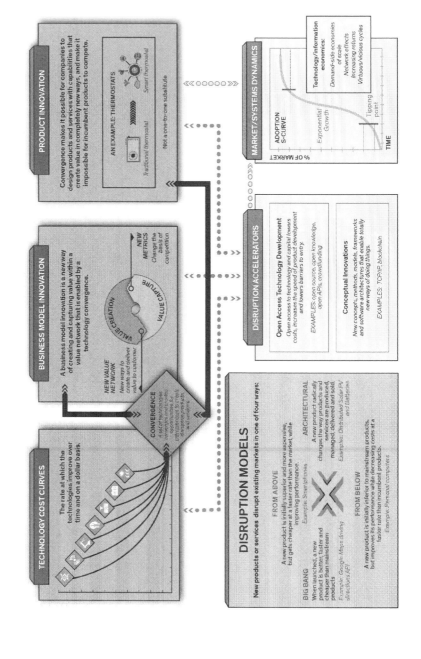

» A primer on the new language of road transportation

The changes sweeping across road transportation are spawning a whole new set of concepts and terminology, including a bewildering array of acronyms. Some (like AV and EV) describe types of vehicles: but others (like TaaS and IO) are shorthand for the business innovations and models that are coming into being.

Box 1: The acronym jungle unpacked

ICE: a vehicle with an Internal Combustion Engine powered with a fuel such as gasoline or diesel.

EV: an Electric Vehicle. In this paper we define EVs as vehicles powered 100% by electric batteries.

AV: an Autonomous Vehicle, or self-driving car. In this paper when we refer to an AV (or an A-EV) we are referring to a fully autonomous vehicle (Level 5) which needs no human intervention at all — or even a steering wheel. This capability is currently an add-on to the underlying vehicle (an ICE or EV) which includes both hardware (sensors and processors) and software (the vehicle operating system).

A-EV: an EV with AV capabilities. In our model all TaaS (see below) vehicles will be A-EVs.

A-ICE: an ICE vehicle with AV capabilities.

Pre-TaaS Platform: this is the online transportation network software infrastructure that manages on-demand transportation by connecting passengers and vehicle drivers via mobile apps. It's also known as ride hailing or ride sharing; companies such as Uber, Lyft and Didi are examples.

TaaS Platform: this is the online transportation network software infrastructure that manages on-demand transportation with fleets of A-EVs.

Vehicle operating system (VOS): the system that controls the vehicle based on artificial intelligence (AI) that takes information from sensors and mapping and drives the vehicle.

Individual ownership (IO): refers to the current model of vehicle ownership, in which vehicles are owned or leased by individuals and travel an average of about 11,300 miles annually.

TaaS: transport-as-a-service. A new model for passengers to access transportation on-demand, providing a level of service equivalent to or higher than current car-ownership models without the need to own a vehicle. In this paper, we use TaaS to refer to services based only on AV technology, delivered by vehicles that are owned by fleet operators and that are used 10× or more per day than IO vehicles.

TaaS Pool: a subset of TaaS that entails sharing a vehicle ride with other people who are not in the passenger's family or social group — the equivalent of today's Uber Pool or Lyft Line. The vehicles delivering TaaS will be the same as TaaS Pool; only their usage (whether passengers are sharing) dictates what they are called. TaaS Pool will eventually grow in numbers of passengers to become more like today's public transportation.

Passenger mile and vehicle mile: the new key metrics for the transportation industry. Both revenues and cost are measured on a per-mile basis. This is in contrast to the conventional car industry, whose revenues are based on "pushing steel" (vehicle units) and after-market sales, while expenses are based on minimizing upfront cost per vehicle unit — regardless of post-sales vehicle utilization.

Cost per vehicle mile and revenues per vehicle mile: key cost and revenue metrics of the TaaS fleet industry.

Cost per passenger mile and revenues per passenger mile: under the basic TaaS model, equivalent to today's taxi, Pre-TaaS (ride hailing), or car ownership models, where the passenger travels individually, cost per passenger mile is equivalent to the cost per vehicle mile. Under TaaS Pool models, the TaaS provider can charge each individual passenger a fraction of the cost per vehicle mile.

» Part 1:
The End of Individual
Car Ownership

» Summary

By 2030, within 10 years of regulatory approval of fully autonomous vehicles, 95% of all U.S. passenger miles will be served by transport-as-a-service (TaaS) providers who will own and operate fleets of autonomous electric vehicles providing passengers with higher levels of service, faster rides and vastly increased safety at a cost up to 10 times cheaper than today's individually owned (IO) vehicles. These fleets will include a wide variety of vehicle types, sizes and configurations that meet every kind of consumer need, from driving children to hauling equipment.

The TaaS disruption will be driven by economics. The average American family will save more than $5,600 per year in transportation costs, equivalent to a wage raise of 10%. As a result, Americans will keep an extra $1 trillion in their pockets, potentially generating the largest infusion of consumer spending in history.

The TaaS disruption will be both quick and inevitable on a global basis. Below, we lay out a baseline analysis of this disruption, followed by a study of its implications for the car and oil industries and a discussion of the choices that society will face.

» 1.1 It's All About the Economics

Our detailed analysis shows that the cost of transport-as-a-service (TaaS) will fall to such an extent that owners of vehicles will abandon their individually owned vehicles at a speed and scale that mainstream analysts have failed to predict (see Box 8). This is because they have failed to foresee the extent of the cost reduction and the impact that will have on the speed of adoption. Mainstream scenarios generally focus on new car sales, with ICE vehicles gradually being replaced by EVs, and not on the entire existing fleet of vehicles being disrupted and stranded.

The TaaS disruption is not just about EVs replacing ICE vehicles when car owners buy new vehicles. Electric vehicles *will* indeed disrupt new ICE vehicle sales — but the TaaS disruption we present in this study is far more profound. Vehicle users will stop owning vehicles altogether, and will instead access them when needed.

The TaaS disruption will end the model of car ownership itself. New car sales and the existing fleet of both ICE and EV vehicles (240 million vehicles in the US) will be displaced as car owners sell or abandon their vehicles and use TaaS.

This disruption will happen largely because of the huge cost savings that *all* individual car owners will have when they choose to stop owning a car and use TaaS instead. In the individual ownership market, drivers face both the upfront costs of buying cars and the ongoing operating costs of using them. With TaaS, all of these costs will be replaced by a single per-usage charge, which will conservatively be two to 10 times cheaper than operating an IO vehicle — and likely far cheaper than that as technologies improve.

Behavioral issues such as love of driving, fear of strangers or habit are generally thought to pose initial barriers to consumer uptake. However, Pre-TaaS companies such as Uber, Lyft and Didi have invested billions of dollars developing technologies and services to overcome these issues. In 2016, Pre-TaaS companies drove 500,000 passengers per day in New York City alone.[5] That was triple the number of passengers driven the previous year. The combination of the dramatically lower cost of TaaS compared with car ownership and exposure to the successful experience of peers will drive more widespread usage of the service. Adopting TaaS requires no investment and does not require any lock-in. Consumers can try it with ease and increase usage as their comfort level increases. Even in suburban and rural areas, where wait times and cost might be slightly higher, adoption is likely to be more extensive than generally forecast because of the greater impact of cost savings on lower income families.

Switching to TaaS will provide Americans with a significant disposable-income boost (equivalent to $5,600 per household on average) — a permanent decrease of living costs. This will have a positive impact on household savings, especially as many Americans have seen very little real wage growth in a generation. For the first time in history, all consumers will have access to cheap and readily available road transport, without having to buy a car. Geographically, the switch will happen first in high-density cities with high real-estate values, such as San Francisco and New York. Early adopters will likely include the young, disabled, poor, elderly and middle-income populations who don't have access to convenient and affordable transportation, as well as those whose opportunity cost is high and who value the time freed by not driving as an income-generating opportunity rather than solely as a cost-saving benefit.

All TaaS vehicles will be autonomous (AVs) based on EV technology (A-EVs) (see Box 3). These vehicles will drive themselves with no human mechanical input (no pedals or steering wheel) and will offer both far lower cost and better service (utility) for the consumer — with no requirement to drive, park, maintain, insure or fuel the vehicle. TaaS will be available on-demand and offer faster travel times and the ability to do other things during a journey. These vehicles will have order-of-magnitude higher asset utilization, leading to a far lower cost-per-mile than individually owned vehicles.

Big bang disruption

The start of this disruption will be the date that AVs are approved for widespread use on public roads. This date is dependent on both technological readiness and regulatory approval. Our analysis indicates that 2021[6] is the most likely date for the disruption point. The TaaS disruption will be what is called a "Big Bang Disruption": The moment that TaaS is available, it will outcompete the existing model in all markets. **We find that within 10 years from this point, 95% of US passenger miles will be traveled by TaaS.**

Cost is the most important factor in consumer choice

The cost differential between car ownership and TaaS will override all other factors that affect consumer choice and ensure that TaaS will be adopted wherever and whenever it is available.

Our demand hypothesis for consumer adoption of new technology is comprised of three elements:

‣ The greater the improvement in cost or utility, the more likely people will adopt a new technology, as long as other factors do not outweigh cost (see below);

‣ The greater the difference in cost or utility, the more weight that factor plays in the decision relative to other factors; and

‣ The scale of the cost savings in relation to disposable income is important. The option of spending about $3,400[7] a year on driverless TaaS journeys (or $1,700 on TaaS Pool), rather than an average of approximately $9,000[8] a year on a personally owned ICE or EV produces a very significant increase in disposable income. This $5,600 cost difference will widen as TaaS adoption increases and the IO ICE industry faces a death spiral.

Given the importance of economics, we begin our report by highlighting the key elements of our cost analysis. Part 1 is a summary of our analysis and findings. Appendix A provides a more detailed view of our analysis.

» 1.2 The Costs of TaaS

Figure 2 provides an overview of our findings of the cost of different transport options that consumers will face over time, as the TaaS disruption unfolds.

Figure 2. Consumer Choices: cost-per-mile analysis[9]

Sources: Authors' calculations based on data from Edmunds, Kelley Blue Book, Your Mechanic, U.S. Department of Energy, U.S. Department of Transportation, U.S. Bureau of Labor Statistics and uSwitch. See Appendix A for further details on the methodology

» IO ICE, IO EV and TaaS costs

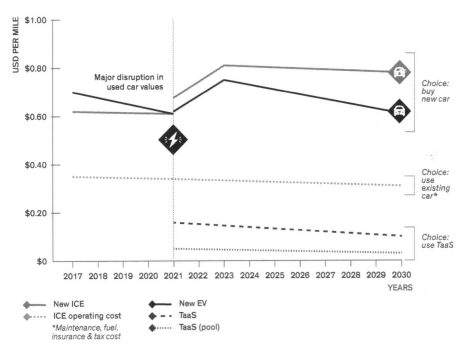

Copyright © 2017 **RethinkX**

Box 2: Cost of transport choices

Based on our model, these are the costs-per-mile of the choices that individual consumers will face as the TaaS disruption unfolds. Consumers will face these choices on day one (the disruption point):

Buy a new car

- ICE: 65 cents (2021), rising to 78 cents[10] (2030)
- EV: 62 cents, falling to 61 cents

Use paid-off existing ICE vehicles

- Operating cost only of ICE: 34 cents, falling to 31 centsto 3 cents

Use TaaS

- TaaS: 16 cents, falling to 10 cents
- TaaS Pool: 5 cents,[11] falling to 3 cents

Annual savings per vehicle in 2021:

- TaaS vs. driving paid-off existing ICE: $2,000
- TaaS vs. new ICE: $5,600

Why is TaaS so cheap?

40% TaaS vehicle utilization, 10 times higher than IO vehicle utilization. Individually owned cars are used only 4% of the time. While there will be fewer cars, TaaS vehicles will be available on-demand 24 hours per day, providing door-to-door transport to passengers. As a result, TaaS vehicles will be utilized 10 times more than IO vehicles.

TaaS vehicles will drive 500,000 miles over their lifetimes — 2.5 times more than ICEs. This dramatically lowers depreciation costs-per-mile, the largest cost component. Each mile covered by a TaaS vehicle costs just 1/500,000th of the upfront cost of the vehicle in depreciation. Because of the low utilization rate of IO vehicles, even an IO EV that is technically capable of driving 500,000 miles will rarely drive more than about 140,000 miles over its lifetime. Dividing upfront costs by 500,000 miles is the single biggest cost-saving item for TaaS vehicles compared to the cost-per-mile of purchasing a new individually owned ICE or EV (see Appendix A).

TaaS vehicles significantly reduce other operating costs. A-EV vehicles are intrinsically more reliable and efficient than ICE vehicles, which leads to major savings in operating costs. These cost reductions include a **90% decrease** in finance costs, an **80% decrease** in maintenance costs, a **90% decrease** in insurance costs and a **70% decrease** in fuel costs. Our extensive primary research, which included data gathering and discussions with operators and manufacturers of EVs, corroborates this finding (see Appendix A for detailed analysis).

These three points have largely been overlooked in most mainstream analyses, which have failed to account for the economic impact of the improved lifetimes of A-EVs and the scale of the operating-cost reductions.

The assumptions behind this cost analysis are conservative, and further potential reductions are possible. We have also conducted a sensitivity analysis of our cost figures. This is summarized in Box 4 below. This means that the cost-per-mile of TaaS could be as low as 6.8 cents per mile on disruption day. That would mean a 10-fold cost advantage over IO ICE the first day that TaaS is introduced — with further cost improvements widening that gap over time.

Box 3: A-ICE vs. A-EV for fleets

TaaS providers will choose A-EVs over A-ICEs

The key initial choice facing TaaS fleet operators is either to use A-EVs or to seek to place autonomous functionality into an ICE (A-ICE). It is likely that some ICE manufacturing companies will offer A-ICE in their fleets to preserve their existing ICE manufacturing investments. The comparison of costs in Figure 3 shows that A-EVs are far cheaper to operate. Furthermore, they offer greater reliability, reducing down-time or outages. We therefore predict that all TaaS vehicles will be A-EVs.

Figure 3. Relative costs-per-mile of A-ICEs vs. A-EVs[12]

Sources: Authors' calculations. For further details see Appendix A

» A-ICE vs. A-EV as basis for fleet choice in 2021

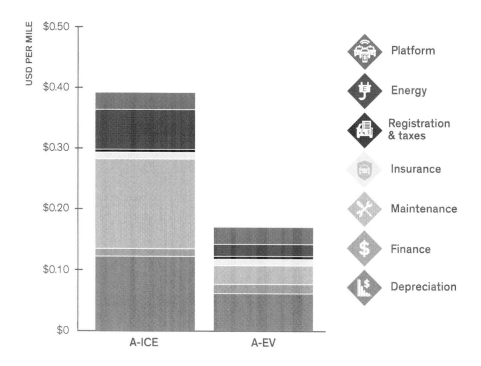

Copyright © 2017 **RethinkX**

Box 4: Sensitivity analysis for 2021 TaaS vehicle (in cents per vehicle mile for TaaS)

	CONSERVATIVE CASE	CENTRAL CASE	UPSIDE CASE
Upfront cost (depreciation) – increase/decrease of $10k per vehicle	+2.0c	6.0c	-2.0c[1]
Vehicle lifetime	+1.0c[2]	500,000 miles	-2.4c[3]
Maintenance	+0.7c[4]	2.9c	-1.5c[5]
Insurance - conservative	+1.3[6]	0.9c	-0.0c
Tax	+1.0c[7]	0.3c	-0.0c
Platform fee	+1.3c[8]	2.6c	-2.6c[9]
Fuel	+0.0c	1.8c	-0.0c
Finance	+1.3c[10]	1.3c	-0.6c[11]
Total cost per vehicle mile	24.5c	15.9c	6.8c

1   This is possible by designing TaaS-specific vehicles based on modularized platform.

2   Battery life of only 200,000 miles — two battery replacements but the rest of vehicle lasting 600,000 miles.

3   Vehicle lifetime of 1,000,000 miles with one battery replacement after 500,000 miles at cost of $100/kWh in 2026.

4   Maintenance increasing to 25% of ICE equivalent.

5   Maintenance decreasing to 10% of ICE equivalent. This is possible now, but further gains from automating process and redesigning vehicles and consumables for resilience could easily deliver these gains.

6   Based on current Tesloop projected cost-per-mile (in a human-driven vehicle).

7   Based on full recovery of gasoline taxes lost.

8   Based on Platform rising to 30% of cost-per-mile.

9   Based on open source platform provided for free (possibly to capitalize on other revenue generating opportunities — the Facebook/Google model).

10   Based on rate of interest rising to 10% per year.

11   Based on rate of interest dropping to 4% per year and utilization of vehicle increasing to 60%.

The disruptive implications of the massive cost difference between TaaS and IO vehicles include:

New car market disrupted by TaaS

From the introduction of TaaS, consumers considering the purchase of a new car will be faced with new economics, in which choosing TaaS over IO will lead to a four- to ten-times reduction in costs. We know of no other market where a 10× cost differential has not led to a disruption. This very significant cost differential will be the key driver for rapid and widespread TaaS adoption for car owners. Potential car buyers will stop buying new cars. This will drive a rapid decline in production of new cars.

As the volume of new car sales falls, revenues will shrink and profits will drop even further. A vicious cycle will ensue, leading to factory closures and consolidation of production. The consequences of a shrinking industry will include a loss of economies of scale, which will lead to higher manufacturing costs for ICE vehicles.

Companies may respond by seeking to raise prices as their cash flows come under pressure. However, as more car owners sell their vehicles and opt for TaaS, the supply of used cars will increase. Today's potential buyers of used cars (young adults, the poor, the middle class family who wants a second or third car) will have already opted for TaaS, thus decreasing potential demand for used cars. The result of increased supply and reduced demand is that the resale value of all used cars will plummet. This "systems dynamic," or feedback loop, will mean that the differential in cost between a new and a used car will increase dramatically, making buying a new car an increasingly unattractive option even for those who still want to buy one. The death spiral of the ICE car industry will thus go into high gear. These factors explain the increase in cost-per-mile of new ICE vehicles between 2020 and 2023 as the TaaS disruption unfolds (Figure 2).

Existing stock of vehicles disrupted by TaaS

Our cost-per-mile analysis indicates that, although the gain for existing car owners from switching to TaaS is less than that for new car purchasers, it is still substantial. If you consider only the operating cost of a vehicle, there will be a two- to four-times cost reduction between driving a paid-off vehicle and switching to TaaS. That is, even if car owners write off the value of their cars and count only the costs of fuel, maintenance and insurance of their existing vehicles, switching to TaaS would still be 50% cheaper than using an individually owned vehicle. Switching to TaaS Pool increases the cost savings to 75%. As a result, we expect increasing proportions of vehicle owners to sell their used cars and move to TaaS, leading to stranding of unused vehicles. It should also be noted that there is a fixed cost element to car ownership, including insurance, road tax and depreciation costs. These costs all increase (per mile) if fewer miles are driven annually (for example, where passengers use a combination of TaaS and continued ownership of a vehicle). Therefore, as annual mileage for an IO vehicle declines, the cost-per-mile goes up, increasing the economic incentive to sell the vehicle and switch completely to TaaS. We also note that there are other potential TaaS gains (See Box 6) that we do not include in our model.

This report shows a conservative model using proven numbers based on existing technology. Using the more aggressive cost assumptions in our sensitivity analysis would lead to a TaaS cost-per-mile of 6.8 cents on day one (disruption point), further increasing the cost differential with individual ownership. This would enable an even faster disruption than we model here.

Box 5: Tesloop case study[13]

Tesloop is a California-based company offering a low-cost alternative to both short-haul aviation and long-distance drives. It currently operates a number of routes around Southern California (e.g., LA to Palm Springs, Las Vegas, etc.), offering door-to-door and pickup-point-based ride sharing service using Tesla cars. Tesloop is utilizing these cars for more than 17,000 miles per month — a level unprecedented for passenger vehicles — and that is expected to rise to 25,000, running or charging them almost 20 hours per day. Tesloop's early data indicates that mainstream assumptions significantly underestimate vehicle lifetime miles and overestimate maintenance and other operating costs-per-mile. Key highlights:

More vehicle lifetime miles, lower operating costs

- **Vehicle lifetime miles.** Tesloop's first vehicle (Tesla S) is now 20 months old and has clocked over 280,000 miles. It reached 200,000 miles with only 6-7% battery degradation.[14] Tesloop's two other vehicles have reached 100,000 miles with degradation of only 7-9%. This is with a very aggressive charge cycle, which CEO Rahul Sonnad describes as "maybe the worst possible behavior patterns given the current battery chemistry optimizations."[15]

  Sonnad expects that these vehicles could easily stay in service for 5 years at 25,000 miles per month — equating to 1.5 million highway miles.[16] The drivetrain and battery are expected to outlast other elements in the vehicle, which may need refurbishment. The current ranges of Model S and Model X vehicles would allow a company such as Tesloop to provide point-to-point (Pre-TaaS) service between Boston and New York City, Austin and Dallas/Fort Worth, or Nashville and Memphis.

- **Maintenance costs.** The cost of tires dominates maintenance costs. Other costs incurred relate to failures in areas such as air conditioning and door handles.[17] As incentives for the manufacturers change toward long-life design, these costs are expected to be minimized, and there is a clear trajectory of lower maintenance in newer vehicles of the same model.

- **Cost-per-mile.** Including maintenance, fuel, insurance, depreciation and finance costs, but excluding driver cost, Tesloop's current cost per vehicle mile is 20 to 25 cents per mile in a Tesla Model S.

The impact of autonomous technology

▸ Tesloop expects driver costs to fall substantially as vehicles reach the technical capability to see Level 4 automation (the penultimate stage before full automation, Level 5). Tesloop has experimented with a business model enabling frequent passengers to book the driver's seat after they receive "pilot training," thus enabling them to travel for free in exchange for providing customer service and taking on emergency driving in unexpected situations.

▸ This would reduce the reliance in our model on full approval of Level 5 automation as a key pre-condition for TaaS, particularly on city-to-city routes, where the need to move cars without any occupants is less important.

▸

What this means in the market

▸ Sonnad makes a few more points: "Beyond the specific cost structure advantages, there is something more profound happening here. When you take away 99% of accident risk, it changes the scalability of TaaS. When you take away not just the maintenance cost, but unexpected downtime, it enables high availability. But most importantly, there is a paradigm shift happening where vehicles are becoming servers. We can digitally monitor them with near-perfect accuracy, and soon we will be able to control them remotely. Human training and human error are no longer paramount. And costs are coming down by a significant percentage year over year for the first time. Maybe that is just 5% or 10% yearly decline, but compared to trains, buses, airlines and gas cars, that's a curve that only leads in one direction. When you combine autonomy, electric drivetrains, deep connectivity and supercharging, you've got — for the first time ever — an almost fully electric/digital system that can move atoms, not just bits."

The road to free transport

TaaS Pool will be cheaper and more convenient than most forms of public transportation. This will not only blur the distinction between public and private transportation but will also most likely lead to a virtual merger between them. We expect that TaaS vehicles will be largely differentiated by size, with two-, four- or eight-seaters and up to 20- or even 40-seaters in the TaaS Pool market. There is potential for the cost to the user (5 cents per TaaS Pool passenger mile in 2021) to be substantially lowered — either through new revenue sources (see below) that will be largely passed on to consumers in the form of lower costs or through further cost reductions not modeled in this analysis. Any remaining cost to the consumer might be covered by corporations or local governments. Corporations might sponsor vehicles or offer free transport to market goods or services to commuters (e.g., "Starbucks Coffee on wheels"[18]). Many municipalities will see free TaaS transportation as a means to improve citizens' access to jobs, shopping, entertainment, education, health and other services within their communities.

Note that we have not included the value of people's time freed from driving. We analyze this in Part 3.

Box 6: Additional factors potentially driving TaaS prices lower

Other revenue sources. A-EVs could generate additional revenue streams, including from charges for entertainment, advertising, monetization of data, and sales of food and beverages. These would create more revenue for fleet owners, which in turn could be either used to reduce the cost of travel for consumers or retained as profit. As an example, advertising revenue based on 12 trillion passenger minutes in TaaS in 2030, with a captive audience and access to data about where they are going and who they are, could lead to highly targeted and valuable digital advertising space.

Grid back-up support. A-EVs could be used to provide back-up support for the U.S. and other national grids in times of peak demand. In our scenario, there will be 20 million TaaS vehicles in the U.S. in 2030, each with 60kWh batteries, resulting in a total of 1,200GWh of battery capacity. The peak draw on the US electricity grid changes between 475GW and 670GW in winter and summer, respectively.[19] In times of peak electricity demand and low transport demand, A-EVs could be programmed to plug in and provide grid support.

Second life of batteries. Our analysis shows that after 500,000 miles, the batteries of A-EVs will still retain 80% of their capacity, which could be reused for grid storage. With 4 million A-EVs retiring annually, the surplus battery power could add 200 GWh of electricity storage to the grid each year.[20] For comparison, the U.S. had 24.6 GW of energy storage in 2013.[21]

Efficiency gains in A-EV design and manufacture. TaaS fleet operators will be strongly incentivized by the potential size of their marketplace, which is likely to lead them to seek to achieve cost efficiencies throughout their supply chains. We therefore expect to see the prioritization of low-cost manufacture, ease of construction and maintenance in A-EVs.

Cheaper manufacture, more miles per A-EV. Competition between A-EV manufacturers may lead to lower upfront costs for TaaS fleet operators, through common modularized vehicle architectures and lower depreciation costs. A-EVs may have lifetimes greater than 500,000 miles as a result of ongoing innovation in autonomous technology, also leading to lower cost-per-mile.

Reduced maintenance costs. To outcompete other operators, there will be market incentives to drive down the costs of maintenance. Cost reduction can be made through the modularization of assembly and replacement parts, and through the automation of maintenance to save labor costs. Consumables will be designed for durability and lifetime, not for planned obsolescence.

Vehicle differentiation. The drive to lower production costs will lead to a standard hardware platform (consisting of the vehicle powertrain platform plus the vehicle operating system computing platform). However, this standard hardware configuration will allow manufacturers to offer a limitless variation in shape, type and performance from three-wheelers to performance cars to trucks and buses.

Cost savings relating to safety factors. As autonomous vehicles gain a bigger market share and safety improves dramatically, hardware requirements that were engineered under the assumption that there would be millions of car crashes per year will be less important. Metal that was used to increase vehicles' body strength and weight will be shed, resulting in lower manufacturing costs.

» 1.3 Systems Dynamics

Systems dynamics drive adoption faster and further

In common with other technology-driven disruptions such as digital cameras, mobile phones and microwave ovens, the shift to TaaS will follow the technology-adoption lifecycle — that is, it will be non-linear, following an S-curve.[22] The exponential nature of adoption is driven, in large part, by the effects of interacting systems dynamics, including a range of feedback loops, market forces and network effects. It cannot be assumed that technology costs drop and adoption increases while "all else remains equal," as mainstream analyses do.

As adoption progresses, certain tipping points are reached where these dynamics affect the cost or utility of competing technologies, leading to an increasingly competitive TaaS marketplace. TaaS becomes progressively cheaper and improves its functionality, while ICE vehicles become ever more expensive to operate and harder to use. We describe below how some of these systems dynamics will operate over the adoption lifecycle.

A fast start in cities

At the outset of the disruption the policy, business and consumer drivers that we describe below will ensure that demand for TaaS exists, that a sufficient supply of vehicles is available, and that a supportive, enabling regulatory framework is created. Markets will reward providers that supply vehicles with long lifetimes and low operating costs, which will both disrupt the basis of competition of the conventional car industry and trigger further cost savings.

TaaS adoption lifecycle reaches critical mass and tipping point

In cities where population density and real estate prices are high (e.g., New York, San Francisco, Boston, Singapore, London) TaaS adoption will likely proceed fastest. Pent-up demand from groups that are not served by the current IO market or have little or no disposable income will ensure that there are many early adopters of TaaS (the disabled, pensioners living on fixed incomes,[23] millennials paying a large proportion of income on rent,[24] middle-class families struggling to stay in cities[25]).

These users will build the critical mass for the TaaS market to reach a tipping point at about 10-20% of the passenger transport market. In line with the technology adoption lifecycle S-curve, once the market reaches this tipping point, demand accelerates, creating a virtuous cycle of more availability of TaaS vehicles, lower costs, higher quality of service, quicker pick-ups and faster rides. This will both increase usage from existing users (i.e., they will use it not only to go to work but also to go to the supermarket or pick up kids at school) and attract even more new users, further propelling the virtuous cycle.

Think of how the digital camera disrupted film cameras. The more early adopters used digital cameras, the more services became available for digital imaging (Flickr, Shutterfly) and the cheaper digital cameras became, which attracted even more users and more ecosystem providers (Facebook, Instagram) which attracted still more mainstream users, and eventually even the more ardent lovers of film cameras put them aside for the vastly cheaper and superior functionality offered by digital imaging.

The flip side of the virtuous cycle of the disruptor is the vicious cycle of the disrupted. The IO ICE industry will enter a vicious cycle that includes plunging new car sales and used car values.

Vicious cycle making the demise of IO vehicles inevitable

As the early majority (mainstream market) adopts TaaS, the IO ICE industry will enter a vicious cycle that will disrupt the industry. Individual car owners will use their ICE vehicles less and less until they stop using them altogether. Early adopters who were car owners will sell their cars and not buy new ones. As TaaS penetration approaches the mainstream point (50%), a critical mass of users will stop using ICE cars, try to sell them and not consider buying a new one. Gas stations, repair shops and dealers will close, first in the cities and then in the suburbs. This will make it even more expensive and time-consuming for the remaining IO ICE drivers to have their cars fueled and serviced. The cost of operating IO ICE cars will keep rising, and the hassle of fueling them in gas stations farther and farther away from home will increase, while the cost of

TaaS will drop and its convenience increase. This will further widen the cost difference and convenience differential between TaaS and IO ICE, which will attract more users who will abandon their cars. More gas stations, repair shops, and dealers will shut down, further pushing the vicious cycle of the ICE industry. Spare parts will become more expensive and more difficult to source as suppliers shut down. Insurance costs for human drivers will rise as the data-driven insurance industry can price premiums according to actual driving patterns, making IO ICE even more expensive to operate. Speed of travel will pick up and congestion decrease because of TaaS, and soon it will become clear that humans are dangerous drivers and are slowing traffic down. Social pressure will lead to calls for legislation to limit areas or times where human drivers are allowed. Furthermore, demand for access to the benefits of TaaS from consumers in areas that are late in the adoption cycle will drive supply to expand and force regulators to consider universal-access measures. At this point, near total adoption of TaaS becomes inevitable as these systems dynamics ensure that IO vehicles are ever more expensive and difficult to operate, and the supply of TaaS reaches even the most rural communities.

Stakeholder dynamics

Disruption happens dynamically within the context of choices made by key stakeholders: consumers, businesses and policymakers. These groups are interdependent, and decisions by any group affect the decisions of the others. Understanding the process of disruption requires insight into the likely behavior of these stakeholders. Below, we summarize our analysis of the key factors that will influence the behavior of each group.

Consumers will be motivated by cost above all else

Demand for TaaS, not supply, will be the key driver of disruption. The scale of the cost differential will override all other factors that influence consumer choice. Many of the perceived barriers to TaaS will be overcome as consumers are exposed to and experience A-EVs. Experimenting by taking a journey in a TaaS vehicle requires no investment other than downloading a phone application, and there are no penalties for taking one journey. The service can be tried at will and the option to cease to use TaaS is always available (it has high "trialability"[26]). TaaS and IO models are also not mutually exclusive;

individual ownership and use of an ICE or EV can continue, alongside use of TaaS. Figure 4 summarizes the key factors that affect consumer choice.

The importance of other factors will vary by consumer, but in the face of 10-fold cost improvements leading to free or nearly free transportation, cost will be the overriding factor in consumer choice. Over time the reasons for initial resistance will diminish, and the appreciation of the economic gains and the improvement in lifestyle and other factors of consumer choice will increase, driven by systems dynamics which tilt the playing field ever further in favor of TaaS.

Figure 4. Summary of factors affecting consumer choice between TaaS and IO

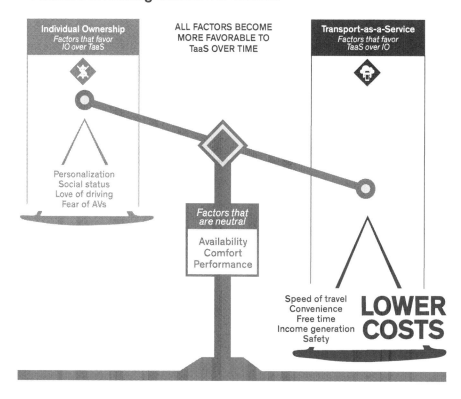

» *Factors affecting consumer choice*

Individual Ownership
Factors that favor IO over TaaS

ALL FACTORS BECOME MORE FAVORABLE TO TaaS OVER TIME

Transport-as-a-Service
Factors that favor TaaS over IO

Personalization
Social status
Love of driving
Fear of AVs

Factors that are neutral

Availability
Comfort
Performance

Speed of travel
Convenience
Free time
Income generation
Safety

LOWER COSTS

Copyright © 2017 RethinkX

Business environment will favor low-cost TaaS

The sheer scale of the potential TaaS market (6 trillion passenger miles in 2030) and the competitive market dynamics will ensure that the supply of vehicles follows demand and that the price of TaaS trends toward cost.[27] Businesses in this market are likely to face the following dynamics:

› A winners-take-all marketplace is likely to emerge, driven by the platform network effects, as TaaS providers compete for the vast per-mile market (**4 trillion US passenger miles** at the TaaS disruption point, rising to **6 trillion** 10 years out).

› These effects are likely to lead to a market-share grab, as TaaS providers look to seize dominance of local markets by flooding the market with vehicles.

› Cost per passenger mile will be a key metric, with market forces rewarding TaaS providers that drive this down (by lowering upfront costs and operating costs and extending vehicle lifetime miles). In fact, the current market incentives to manufacturers (selling car "units" and making money from repairs) reward the opposite model for lifetime and operating costs, and there are huge potential gains possible here as market forces change.

› Consumers will benefit from low per-mile prices in an intensely competitive marketplace, as prices trend toward cost, with any new income sources created likely to be passed on in the form of lower prices. It is likely that market forces will prevent monopoly pricing power even as oligopolies begin to form (see Box 7).

The existential threat that TaaS will pose to incumbent transport businesses should be a strong motivator for them to try to reinvent themselves, either as hardware (vehicle) manufacturers or as TaaS providers. The multi-trillion-dollar potential market opportunities in TaaS will also attract new entrants. In such a competitive market, it will initially be difficult for TaaS providers to secure monopolistic returns, and the consumer will benefit as any alternative sources of revenue are passed on. Competitive markets lead to prices trending toward cost. We expect highly competitive pricing, and perhaps even price wars and short-term loss-leader pricing as providers look to secure dominance in local markets. Over time, this dynamic will reverse, as winners begin to emerge and local markets become defined by the winners. We do not expect the winning platform providers to have the ability to impose monopoly pricing (see Box 7).

Box 7: Monopoly pricing?

Platform network effects: Pre-TaaS platforms such as Uber benefit from network effects. The more passengers the platform has, the more drivers it attracts, which leads to a virtuous cycle of shorter wait times and quicker rides for passengers, which leads to more passengers signing up, which leads to more drivers, and so on. The value of the platform increases with each additional driver and user. This two-sided network (drivers and passengers) forces a winner-take-all dynamic. In the end, there is only room for a small number of platforms in each geographic market. There are concerns that this dynamic will lead to a monopoly situation, with the winners able to charge monopoly prices to consumers and not pass on the cost savings. Our analysis suggests that this will not be the case in most markets.

The current Pre-TaaS platforms are two-sided markets. Drivers and users create network effects. The more drivers (cars), the more users, and vice versa. However, even now this network effect is mitigated by drivers working for multiple platforms (Lyft and Uber) at the same time, and by passengers having access to several apps.

Platform providers compete for a limited supply of drivers by offering incentives and charging a smaller platform fee. Uber has raised its platform fee, while Lyft has lowered it. Thus Lyft can attract more drivers and attempt to enable its own virtuous cycle.

The dynamics of Pre-TaaS favor a small number of providers in each geographic market (more mutually exclusive platforms means worse service and increased wait times). There is concern that these network effects will allow the "winners" to adopt monopoly prices as the market consolidates into a few providers. However, this dynamic does not translate into market pricing power. Each city is essentially its own local market, and any competitor (an investor, manufacturer or platform company) could purchase a local fleet and undercut the monopoly pricing. This dynamic would ensure that prices remain competitive and not monopoly-based.

The platform technology is based largely on software. This software will be developed by many companies seeking to win local markets — for instance, Didi in China, Uber and Lyft in the U.S., Ola in India, and Grab in Southeast Asia. The capability to use this software to enter new markets will be there and hence does not represent a barrier to entry. We would also expect a robust Android-like open source version to be available. In fact, Waze, a Google company, is offering a ride-hailing service that is competitive with Uber in several cities. LibreTaxi, a San Francisco-based startup, is offering free open source ride-hailing software. Anybody anywhere can download and use it for free and potentially become an instant competitor to existing market leaders like Uber.

The Pre-TaaS two-sided network effects will disappear once AVs are introduced, since no human drivers are needed. Barriers to entry into TaaS will thus fall, which will open up opportunities for new entrants. Both TaaS software and fleets of A-EVs will be readily available to enter new markets without the need to invest in recruiting drivers. This will prevent abusive market pricing behavior by the winning providers in most markets.

Platform providers will make money from volume, not margin. They will add new sources of revenues (for instance, vehicles might move goods when they are not moving people), new business-model innovations (for instance, charge video streaming services a fee to be an exclusive provider over the platform), and more product lines (drones as a service, perhaps) to increase the value of the network.

An analogy is Amazon Web Services (AWS), which is by far the largest cloud service provider in the world. It has consistently lowered prices in line with decreases in the cost of computing. It has not abused its market position even though thousands of companies depend on AWS for their information technology needs. Instead, AWS has expanded the range of products and services it offers, providing customers even more sources of revenues and value. The threat of deep-pocket technology competition from Microsoft, Google and IBM keeps Amazon from abusing its market position.

Policymakers can help accelerate or delay the transition to TaaS

Policymakers will face several critical junctures when their decisions will either help accelerate or delay the transition to TaaS. The first and most critical decision is whether to remove barriers at the national level, or by city or state. A national approach would be far faster. The U.S. government pledged $4 billion to accelerate the development of self-driving cars on a national basis.[28] The National Highway Traffic Safety Administration (NHTSA) has already started developing a "framework for the safe and rapid deployment of these advanced technologies."[29]

But California is not waiting for the federal government. The Golden State, home to many of the companies leading the AV disruption, such as Google, Tesla and Uber, has, at the time of publication, approved requests by 30 companies[30] to test their self-driving cars on public roads and has proposed rules to allow fully autonomous (Level 5) vehicles as soon as this year.[31]

Many policymakers will be driven to act by the economic, social and environmental benefits of TaaS, including:

‣ **Technology leadership gains** as countries, states, and cities vie to gain first-mover advantage in the development of technologies within the A-EV supply chain. **Leadership here will ensure that businesses in these jurisdictions will be best placed to lead the disruption globally and capture the wealth and job creation associated with it.**

‣ **Productivity gains** from freeing up of time to work during commutes and faster transport times for consumers, leading to an increase in GDP of $500 billion to $2.5 trillion (see Part 3).

‣ **Consumer income gains**, which we estimate as equivalent to a tax cut or income gain of $5,600 per household on average[32] per year from 2021 or $1 trillion annually in total in 2030. Consumer spending is by far the largest driver of the economy, comprising about 71% of total GDP.[33]

‣ **Public sector budget gains** from lower highway infrastructure costs and from the possibility of a "land bonanza" as publicly owned land within road right of ways is freed up for other uses.

‣ **Quality of life gains** from improved mobility for those who are unable to drive themselves, access to transport for those who cannot afford it, cleaner air, fewer road fatalities and injuries, and the increased ability of governments to meet their climate change targets.

Policy might be driven at a federal level or state-by-state or city-by-city. Supportive federal policy would help to fast-track the transition; however, it is not a pre-condition. As some cities lead this process, the benefits of low-cost accessible transportation will become so evident that policymakers elsewhere will face business and societal pressure to fast-track the transition. We expect to see a competitive policy environment with countries and cities competing to lead the disruption, and thus capture the associated benefits. Support could manifest in incubation for wide-scale pilots, accelerated approval of AV technology, investment in infrastructure, and introduction of clear and simple insurance rules that protect the public and clear legal hurdles holding up AVs.

Conversely, there might be hostility to the driverless TaaS disruption in some jurisdictions for cultural, socio-economic or political reasons, considering that incumbent businesses will suffer losses from the introduction of TaaS. For instance, up to 5 million jobs may be lost, leading to aggregate income losses of $200 billion per year. These losses can be offset both by job gains created elsewhere in the economy that will arise from increases in consumer disposable income and productivity and by job creation associated with global technology leadership. Resistance to TaaS will ensure these new jobs are created elsewhere in the world but will not avoid the job losses due to the disruption. Oil industry revenues will shrink dramatically. We therefore expect that the oil industry will lobby hard against regulatory approval of A-EVs. Those countries or regions that bow to this pressure will face a reduction in their competitive position globally, given the outsized benefits that a TaaS disruption will bring. The countries that dominated the late 20th century global economy (the United States, Japan and Germany) were some of the countries most poised to benefit from the ICE disruption of horse-based transportation earlier that century. Countries that fail to lead or make a transition to TaaS will become the 21st century equivalents of horse-based countries trying to compete with economies whose transportation systems are based on cars, trucks, tractors and airplanes.

All the technologies associated with TaaS are global. The TaaS disruption will be a global disruption. The technology adoption lifecycle suggests that there will be innovators, early adopters, mainstream adopters, late adopters and laggards. If one country, state or city bans or fail to approve AVs, the disruption will still happen, but in another country, state or city. Whatever barriers keep mainstream adopters from A-EVs will be erased as they witness the benefits that accrue to the early adopters. Similarly, the late adopters will follow closely behind the mainstream adopters. The only question about TaaS is who will be the innovators and who will be the laggards, not whether this disruption will happen.

Box 8: The mainstream view of disruption

Key arguments in mainstream analyses

Mainstream analyses predict that individual vehicle ownership will continue as the principal consumer choice — the business-to-consumer model. This is due to a number of reasons, including the belief that "we love our cars" (like we loved our horses), and the fact that these analyses do not perceive the extent of cost savings from switching to TaaS.

Most analyses see both EVs and AVs as one-to-one substitutions for ICE vehicles; that is, in the future, we will choose to own an EV or AV instead of an ICE.

Mainstream scenarios model autonomous technology as a feature, like rustproofing or alloy wheels, for individually owned cars. For instance, they envision an AV that would take a consultant from home to work, after which she would send her car back to park at home and wait to be called back to pick her up after work. This AV would still be parked 96% of the time.

EVs are seen as a disruption from above, with superior but more expensive EVs falling in price over time, leading to a shift from new ICE vehicle sales to new EV sales. Mainstream analyses envision the existing global fleet of a billion ICE cars would take decades to replace, with ICE sales continuing into the 2040s and beyond.34

Price comparisons between ICEs and EVs are mainly based on the traditional metrics of the conventional car industry, such as upfront costs of purchase (rather than cost-per-mile in TaaS). Vehicle lifetime has little impact on cost, as depreciation is based on residual value, not on lifetime miles.

Mainstream analyses generally see no mass stranding of existing vehicles.

As a result, mainstream forecasts show vehicle disruption as a multi-decadal progression, not as the sharp S-curve exponential shift that would happen quickly and change the business model of the entire industry altogether.

Mainstream analyses generally pay scant attention to the disruption systems dynamics that drive both the 10× cost differential between TaaS and IO ICE and the technology adoption S-curve that wipes out the existing industry.

» 1.4 The Speed and Extent of Adoption

Our model relies on regulation only insofar as it permits the use of Level 5 autonomous vehicles. Further supportive regulation can accelerate the speed of adoption that we model. We assume that adoption is driven by consumer demand, and that supply of TaaS anticipates or closely follows demand, given the size of the opportunity to businesses and the threat to businesses that fail to lead. The TaaS disruption point date of 2021 is a key variable, based on our assessment of technological readiness and regulatory dynamics. Given that key A-EV technologies are improving exponentially, the disruption point could happen sooner in some areas, in 2019 or 2020. The way that the adoption unfolds would not change from the assessment below. It would just happen sooner.

How adoption unfolds: Cities first, then radiating outwards

We see the adoption unfolding over five periods in the timeline:

Phase 0: Pre-Approval

This is happening today. In this period, Pre-TaaS (ride-hailing) companies gain critical masses of passengers and users in major cities around the world. While there is incumbent political opposition in some geographies, the idea of car-as-a-service becomes culturally and politically acceptable, and it even becomes the norm in cities with high population density and high real estate prices. We will see the manufacture of vehicles with fully autonomous capabilities starting as soon as this year. The level of autonomy these vehicles use on the road will depend on regulation, not technological capability. These companies will collect data that will allow them to keep improving their self-driving technology and mapping capabilities on an exponential basis. Pilot projects testing fully autonomous technology increase from a few cities to dozens of cities around the world. Future TaaS providers develop their own self-driving car technology, license self-driving technologies from independent providers, or purchase self-driving technology companies and begin to build fleets in readiness for the disruption point. Legislation is introduced to abolish minimum parking requirements in new buildings in central business districts in cities around the world.

Disruption point

This is the date when widespread approval of autonomous vehicle use on public roads is granted by regulators, which in our model we estimate as 2021.

Phase 1: Early adoption phase, years 1-3.

Pre-TaaS companies convert their fleets to A-EVs and become TaaS providers. Urban users adopt TaaS for an increasing proportion of journeys. A-EVs become accepted by a growing number of mainstream users as exposure to them increases. In cities with the highest density and real estate prices, TaaS quickly begins to provide more passenger miles than IO vehicles. Car owners stop buying new cars and begin to sell their vehicles. Legislation is introduced to ban ICE vehicles and non-autonomous vehicles in central business districts in cities around the world.

Phase 2: Mainstream adoption phase, years 3-8.

TaaS radiates outward beyond larger urban areas toward suburban areas, smaller cities and then rural regions. TaaS providers gradually merge, first in densely populated regions. Increasing numbers of users abandon car ownership altogether. Legislation to ban ICE and non-autonomous vehicles spreads to cities around the world.

Phase 3: Plateau phase, years 8-10.

The role of public transportation authorities will have changed dramatically, from owning and managing transportation assets to managing TaaS providers to ensure equitable, universal access to low-cost transportation. TaaS providers who may have lost the battle for the larger city markets expand into smaller cities and rural areas, filling in the remaining market gaps. Potentially, society will demand that public transportation authorities help provide TaaS availability for the full population, as has happened previously with the provision of telephony, water and electricity.

The speed and extent of adoption

Aggregating our analysis and applying our adoption framework, we conclude that:

▸ **TaaS will provide 95% of U.S. passenger miles within 10 years of the disruption point.**

▸ **This 95% adoption plateau is based on 20-25% of rural users remaining non-adopters (see Box 9).** Market penetration could rise above 95% if the vicious cycle of IO ICE markets lowers the quality and raises the cost of ownership to extreme levels, or if society requires that public transportation authorities provide universal high-quality TaaS service the way we have done in the past with telephone, water and electric services.

▸ **TaaS vehicles are almost 60% of those on roads in 2030.** The 95% mileage figure equates to 60% of vehicles in the U.S. vehicle stock being A-EVs; the remaining 40% will be largely comprised of legacy individually owned ICEs. Our model sees 26 million TaaS vehicles and 18 million IO vehicles in 2030 (See Part 2).

▸ **Rebound in demand.** Overall increase in passenger miles from 4 to 6 trillion. This increase is a function of: i) increases in travel by currently disadvantaged (often non-driving) users such as the elderly, disabled, poor, sick and young; ii) price elasticity and its consequences (lower prices trigger more demand); and iii) "slippage" from other forms of transport such as short-haul aviation, buses and bicycles. It is likely that given the 10-fold decrease in cost, the addition of new demographics and the likelihood of free transportation, 6 trillion passenger miles is an underestimate. If so, this would point to a higher percentage of total miles being TaaS and a faster transition away from IO and ICE.

▸ **Urban TaaS will reach 95% market penetration sooner than the graph shows.** Figure 5 shows adoption for the U.S. as a whole. Urban markets will move faster, and then TaaS will radiate outward to rural areas.

Vehicle supply will meet demand

Our analysis does not foresee supply side constraints affecting the delivery of the necessary vehicles to meet demand. The major risk to this statement lies in the potential bottlenecks in the supply of raw materials, particularly lithium and cobalt. Provided that the market anticipates the scale of disruption, market forces should deliver the required increases in supply of these materials. The increase in utilization of TaaS vehicles means that far fewer vehicles are needed to deliver the supply of passenger miles. Manufacturing or assembly constraints do not represent a barrier to our model. Furthermore, we do not see any other barriers causing this demand-led disruption to be derailed.

TaaS vehicles are essentially EVs with added information-technology hardware and software capabilities; thus, we use EV manufacturing capacity as the basis for our analysis. Assembly capacity, battery capacity and lithium supply are the factors frequently cited as potential supply constraints. Here we provide an outline of why we do not see these issues acting as brakes on the speed and extent of driverless TaaS adoption.

Box 9: The non-adopters

Key arguments in mainstream analyses

Who will be the 5% that do not adopt TaaS after 10 years? These non-adopters fall into three categories: rural consumers, the very rich and tech-laggards.

Rural consumers

We see this group as accounting for the vast majority of non-adopters. Smaller rural communities may not have the population density to have high enough demand to attract a critical mass of TaaS vehicles and maintain a sufficient level of service (in terms of waiting time, for example). This means that there will be many trips where the TaaS vehicle will have to wait for a passenger to take on a return trip or will make a long trip with an empty vehicle to pick up a passenger elsewhere. Waiting time and empty ("deadhead") trips add to the cost-per-mile. There are several ways to ameliorate these issues. Planned trips can be scheduled in advance if a passenger can plan pick-up times (i.e., she works 9 a.m. to 5 p.m. and always has to be picked up at 8 a.m.). Predictive analytics by TaaS providers will become increasingly accurate in predicting when and where TaaS pickups will be required, which will dramatically diminish waiting times. Additionally, there is a credible counter-argument to rural consumers becoming late adopters. Rural populations are generally poorer than urban or suburban populations. The relative cost savings of shifting to TaaS will be far higher for rural families than for the rest of the population.

The very rich

This category is defined as those who are not motivated by road travel economics, despite the scale of the savings that TaaS offers. The closest proxy for this is the proportion of consumers who currently spend over five times the average price for a vehicle.35 The counter argument is that people with high paying jobs may have a bigger incentive to ride a driverless car because they will earn a lot more money by working in the car instead of driving. Either way, this group is small enough that is not material in terms of overall TaaS adoption.

Tech laggards

In this group, we place those who will not switch to TaaS for a range of personal reasons, including dislike of change, distrust of new technology and perceived loss of personal freedom.

It is possible that the feedback loops that will decimate the ICE value chain outlined above will make operating an ICE vehicle far too difficult and expensive, leading to a near-universal adoption of TaaS.

Assembly (vehicle manufacture) capacity.

EV manufacturing capacity is growing, and our forecast is for capacity to far exceed the requirements that we model for TaaS. However, if the growth rate of new specialized EV manufacturing capacity drops dramatically, any assembly shortfall in capacity can be mitigated by conversion of ICE assembly capacity, which can easily be adjusted to produce EVs — which are far simpler to assemble. Companies such as Nissan manufacture EVs and ICE vehicles in the same plants. In fact, a significant portion of assembly happens on the same lines.

Battery manufacturing capacity.

The ability to manufacture the required number of batteries is currently much debated. Factories to produce the batteries are under construction in the U.S. and elsewhere. These factories are relatively easy to scale, with most equipment available off the shelf, so this is unlikely to be a constraint. Discussions with multiple experts suggest that it takes just 9-12 months to build a new battery manufacturing plant able to produce multiple gigawatt-hours of battery capacity.[36]

Mineral supply for batteries.

This is often seen as the potential key supply constraint, as the processes involved in opening a new lithium or cobalt mine and developing the attendant battery-grade refining capacity are complex and can take about three years. But our discussions with mineral experts suggest that the supply volumes required to meet the demand curves shown in our models are achievable. Current global lithium reserves exceed 30 million tons,[37] and our estimates calculate that 1 million tons of lithium will be required, per year, by 2030.[38] For analysis of cobalt supply for batteries, see Part 3.

Figure 5. The Speed of Adoption

Sources: Authors' analysis based on U.S. Department of Transportation data

» *Speed of TaaS adoption*

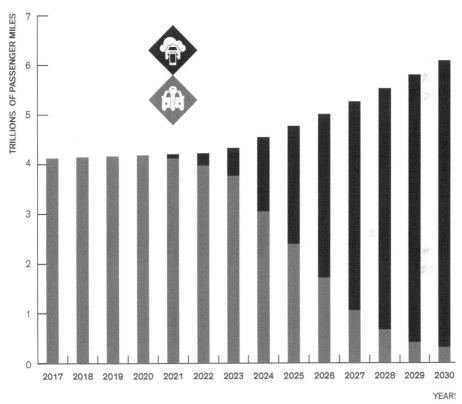

　　　　　　　　　　　　　　　　　　　　　　　　　RethinkTransportation

» Part 2:
TaaS Disruption.
Oil and Auto Value Chains

» Summary

In Part 1, we touched on the likely impacts of the TaaS disruption on vehicle supply chains. This section explores the implications for the auto industry in more detail. We also analyze the disruptive effects of TaaS on the oil value chain.

» 2.1 Introduction

Our research and modeling indicate that the $10 trillion annual revenues in the existing vehicle and oil supply chains will shrink dramatically as a result of the TaaS disruption.[39] As previous market disruptions have shown, the market valuation of companies serving these industries will shrink even more dramatically. There will also be new wealth and jobs generated by TaaS. As in previous disruptions,[40] these gains may not accrue to today's leading industry players.

In this section, we highlight key considerations that stakeholders may want to consider before the TaaS disruption reaches the point of no return.

Our findings point to nuance in the likely outcomes. Some parts of the vehicle value chain will face existential threats and are unlikely to survive; but other parts have the assets, capabilities, and technology to make a transition and even to achieve dominance within the new value chain that will be enabled by the TaaS disruption.

The outlook for the future of oil supply chains is universally bleak, with negative effects for all industry players. However, these negative effects will be disproportionally distributed across countries, companies and oil fields, depending on the cost of production.

Below, we look at the likely impacts of the TaaS disruption and examine the choices that auto manufacturers and oil companies will face. We provide a map of the supply chains (see Figure 6) for background.

Box 10: Value chain summary

Summary points:

The TaaS disruption, as described in Part 1, will have profound implications across the automotive and oil value chains. These include:

• The number of passenger miles will increase from 4 trillion miles in 2015 to 6 trillion in 2030.

• The cost of delivering these miles will drop from $1,481 billion in 2015 to $393 billion in 2030.

• The size of the U.S. vehicle fleet will drop from 247 million in 2020 to 44 million in 2030.

• Annual manufacturing of new cars will drop by 70% during the same period.

• Annual manufacturing of new ICE mainstream cars sold to individuals will drop to zero. Car dealers will cease to exist.

• Huge opportunities will emerge in vehicle operating systems, computing platforms and TaaS fleet platforms.

• Global oil demand will drop from 100 million barrels per day in 2020 to around 70 million barrels per day in 2030.

• The price of oil will drop to around $25 per barrel.

• Oil prices might collapse as soon as 2021.

• High-cost oil fields will be completely stranded.

• Infrastructure dependent on high-cost oil fields, including the Keystone XL and Dakota Access pipelines, will be stranded.

Figure 6. Vehicle and Oil Supply Chains

» Transportation value chain

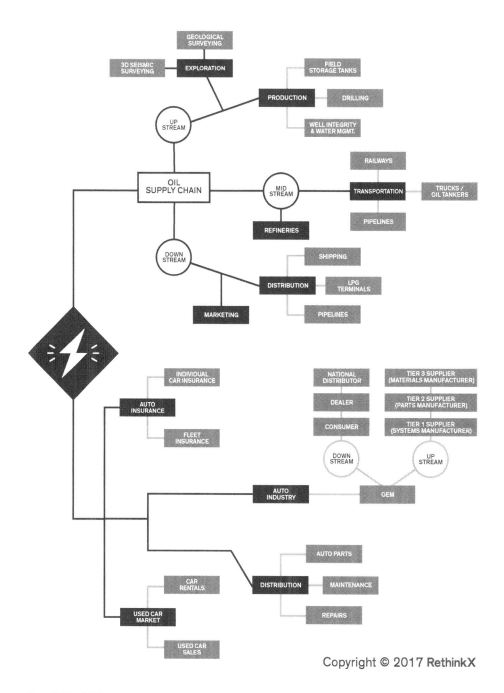

» 2.2 Disruption of the Passenger Vehicle Value Chain

Disruptions, metrics and revenues

History demonstrates that disruptions bring new players — and new metrics.[41] The disruption of road transportation will be no different. The principal metric of the conventional auto industry over the last century has been vehicle units sold; how efficiently they were used was not a salient issue when assessing success.

Figure 7. Revenue distribution along the car value chain

Sources: Authors' calculations based on data from Auto Rental, Edmunds, Kelley Blue Book, Ibis World, Statista, U.S. Bureau of Labor Statistics, U.S. Department of Energy, U.S. Energy Information Administration and the Wall Street Journal

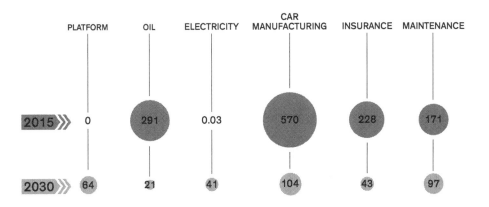

» Revenue distribution along the car value chain in billions of U.S. dollars

	PLATFORM	OIL	ELECTRICITY	CAR MANUFACTURING	INSURANCE	MAINTENANCE
2015	0	291	0.03	570	228	171
2030	64	21	41	104	43	97

The TaaS disruption will bring new metrics. Transportation companies that organize their resources around these key metrics will be best positioned for success, while those that ignore these new metrics will do so at their peril. From the date at which adoption of TaaS begins (the 2021 disruption point in our model), the key unit of measurement[42] will be miles traveled, with four variants as the key indicators: passenger miles, vehicle miles, dollar cost-per-mile and dollar revenues per mile.

Revenues shrinking by two-thirds

We estimate that passenger miles will increase by 50%, from 4 trillion passenger miles in 2015 to 6 trillion passenger miles in 2030. However, the revenues generated will shrink significantly, from around $1.5 trillion in 2015 to $393 billion in 2030 — a decrease of more than 70% (see Figure 7).

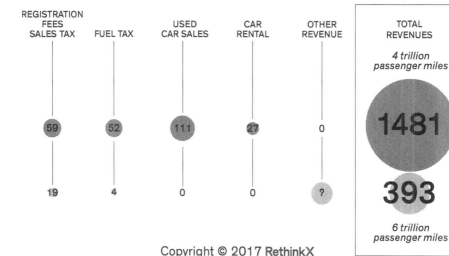

Copyright © 2017 RethinkX

Vehicle fleet size will drop by over 80%, from 247 million vehicles in 2020 to 44 million in 2030. The major driver of a smaller total vehicle stock is increased vehicle asset utilization (see Part I). Just 26 million vehicles will deliver the 5.7 trillion passenger miles traveled via TaaS in the U.S. in 2030, with the remaining 5% of miles attributed to 18 million legacy IO vehicles (see Figure 8).

97 million ICE vehicles[43] will be left stranded in 2030, representing the surplus that will be in the vehicle stock as consumers move to TaaS. These vehicles may eventually become entirely unsellable as used IO vehicle supply soars and demand disappears (see Figure 8).

‣ *New vehicle annual unit sales drop 70% by 2030,* from 18 million in 2020 to 5.6 million in 2030 (see Figure 9). While the number of vehicles in the overall stock drops by 80% over our timeframe, new vehicle sales suffer a slightly lower decline. This is because each vehicle under TaaS is travelling 10 times farther, and hence reaches its end of life more quickly. Vehicles in the TaaS fleet are therefore on a faster replacement cycle (in years) even though they have longer lifetimes (in miles).

‣ *New ICE vehicle sales[44] are finished by 2024,* just three years after the regulatory approval and commercial availability of A-EV technology. In 2024, the pre-existing vehicle stock can more than meet the passenger-mile requirement for transport under individual ownership.

‣ *Used ICE car prices plunge to zero[45] or even negative value.* The rising cost of maintenance, gasoline and insurance; the cost of storing or taxing worthless vehicles; and the lack of a used car market might mean that prices go to zero or even below. That is to say, owners may need to pay to dispose of their cars.

‣ *ICE vehicles eliminated from fleet by end of 2030s at the latest.*[46] Given that the average age of a vehicle on the road is 11.5 years[47], we can expect that ICE cars sold before 2023 must be replaced by the mid-2030s. This means that the remaining ICE vehicles will be eliminated from the fleet before 2040.

‣ *Car dealers cease to exist by 2024,* with no new IO car sales from 2024 onwards and no direct consumer purchases given that TaaS vehicles will be fleet owned.[48]

- *Car insurance will be disrupted[49]* by a 90% fall in the insurance costs incurred by TaaS users (relative to IO), which is driven by the elimination of theft and sharp reductions in insurer costs for liability, injury and vehicle damage.

- *Almost $50 billion in revenues from gasoline taxes will be lost* in the U.S., with the shift from an IO ICE to a shared A-EV fleet.[50] However, governments whose budgets depend on this revenue could shift to taxing miles rather than gasoline or diesel.

Figure 8. Personal vehicle fleet size and composition between 2015 and 2030

Sources: Author's calculations based on U.S. Department of Transportation data

» Projected trends in fleet size and composition

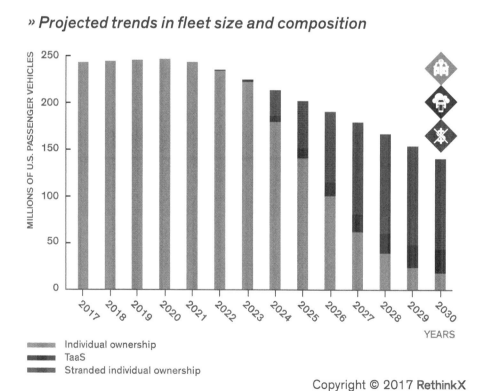

Individual ownership
TaaS
Stranded individual ownership

Areas of opportunity

While TaaS will trigger an enormous disruption, different industries along the vehicle value chain will be subject to disproportional losses and gains. While the commoditization of road passenger travel will drive down hardware margins and volumes, there will also be new opportunities, through the creation of higher-margin businesses in operating systems, TaaS platforms and services, and additional revenue streams, spurred by new business models built upon these platforms. These are outlined briefly, below.

Vehicle operating systems

The companies that develop A-EV operating systems stand to reap massive rewards, as has been the case for Microsoft, Apple, Google and Cisco through their development of computing, internet and smartphone operating systems.[51]

Currently, Tesla's Autopilot is in a dominant position, having been tested for 1.3 billion miles;[52] Tesla's CEO, Elon Musk has stated that all Tesla vehicles will be fully autonomous by the end of 2017.[53] Other early movers include Google (Waymo), NVIDIA, Uber and Baidu. Companies within the incumbent auto industry, such as GM and Ford, have also acquired Silicon Valley startups that are developing autonomous vehicle software.

» ICE vs. TaaS: Projected trends in annual sales

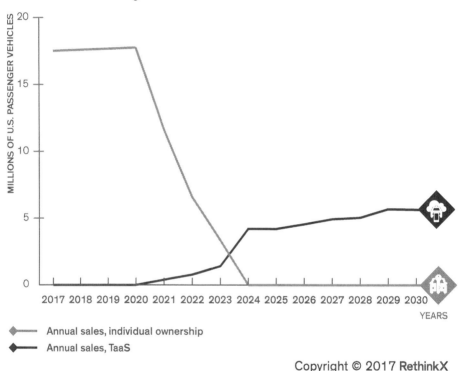

Copyright © 2017 RethinkX

TaaS platforms — a large and growing market opportunity

As with operating systems, TaaS platforms are expected to benefit from network effects: The more users a platform has, the more users it will attract. Once a TaaS platform reaches critical mass, it will become dominant in that market. Companies such as Uber, Lyft and Didi are examples of Pre-TaaS companies that have invested billions to win market share as they evolve toward the driverless A-EV disruption point.

The major difference between operating systems and TaaS platforms is that the network effects for the latter are local or regional. Being the market leader in New York or even in the U.S. does not necessarily translate into winning the same position elsewhere, such as in China or India, as has already been demonstrated in the competition between Uber and Didi in China. Similar dynamics seem to be playing out in India, where Ola is providing intense competition to Uber.

It seems clear that TaaS platforms will be the new transportation brands, as is already evident in the Pre-TaaS era of technology-enabled ride hailing, where consumer relationships are with Uber, Lyft, or Didi rather than with Toyota, General Motors or Volkswagen. The hardware portion of the road passenger transport value chain is thus likely to become commoditized, leading to manufacturer brand-value erosion. This would mirror consumer experience in most internet and social media contexts, where many user relationships are with Facebook, Google or Amazon, not the computer or networking companies which power their data centers.

Tesla's recent announcement about the development of its own ride-sharing platform is an indicator of this future industry trend.[54] Elsewhere, a number of platform-related developments by auto industry incumbents are in progress, including GM's $500 million investment in Lyft,[55] BMW's ride-sharing service, ReachNow,[56] and VW's $300 million investment in Gett.[57]

A key outcome from the development of winning TaaS platforms will be the potential of data generated, to power new products and enhance services still further. The more miles traveled by a company's vehicles, the greater the value of the data.[58]

Tesla's Autopilot is an example where testing its software in real-life vehicles has generated data to improve its semi-autonomous capability. According to an NHTSA report, Tesla crash rates decreased by 40% after it introduced its Autopilot capability in 2015.[59] Looking ahead, TaaS providers will use data derived from vehicle sensors to build mapping data, which could be used either to outcompete others directly, or as the basis of other revenue generation, such as licensing. And, at a more macro level, data from sensors could inform understanding and corresponding actions relating to weather, air quality, human foot traffic and even passenger health.

Computing platform

Intel became one of the biggest market winners of the PC disruption by creating the central processing units (CPUs), which became the platforms for the two prevailing operating systems (MS-DOS and Windows). The TaaS disruption has also created a race to become the "Intel of autonomous vehicles." For example, NVIDIA has invested heavily in repurposing its graphics processing units in order to run the deep learning software that is inherent to AVs. Intel itself recently spent $15 billion to acquire Mobileye, a self-driving technology company, to compete in this market.[60]

Entertainment, work and other opportunities

Americans spend around 140 billion hours in cars every year, a number that will increase by 2030.[61] The TaaS disruption will free up time otherwise spent driving to engage in other activities: working, studying, leisure options and sleeping. This will act as an increase in productivity and provide a boost to GDP (see Part 3.5)

From the TaaS provider perspective, additional services could be offered, such as entertainment (movies, virtual reality), work services (offices on wheels) and food and beverage (Starbucks Coffee on wheels). Providers could act as distributors, earning revenues via a range of business models, including a percentage of sales generated on their platform (as in the Amazon and Apple stores), advertising revenues from onboard entertainment (similar to the Facebook and Google AdWords models), or the as-yet-undeveloped business innovations that are likely to arise from the TaaS disruption.

Implications for vehicle manufacturing companies

Margins in car manufacturing reduced

TaaS will pose formidable challenges for vehicle manufacturers. As consumers shift away from individual ownership, much lower retail ICE and EV unit sales will follow. In our modeling, margins will be reduced as the first mover's advantage dynamics drives TaaS providers to price their services even lower, squeezing supplier margins, and leading to a fall of 80% in manufacturing revenues by 2030 in our model. In parallel, we see further margin reductions from the commoditization of A-EV manufacture. Given these dynamics, value destruction is inevitable.

On commoditization, A-EVs have competitive advantages over ICEs because their powertrains have many fewer moving parts (20 versus 2,000).[62] Further considerations relate to how parts are sourced and standardized. It is not a given that current car manufacturers are best equipped in these contexts. For example, batteries are often manufactured by specialized electronics companies such as Panasonic (battery provider to Volkswagen and Tesla) and Samsung SDI (which provides them for BMW.)[63,64] It may be the case that original equipment manufacturer (OEM) companies will be akin to the electronic manufacturing services (EMS) providers in the communications industry (e.g., Foxconn's role in the assembly of Apple iPhones). On standardization, the most likely pathway is for a base design that can be adapted to different vehicle sizes. Optional high margin extras such as rustproofing, extended warranties and paint proofing will become obsolete.

Taking these factors into account, we estimate an 8% manufacturing margin for OEMs. This may be conservative. If assembly moves closer to the electronic-products model, margins could be closer to 4%. Margins could fall further still if TaaS providers bypass vehicle OEMs and purchase directly from service companies, such as Magna, Continental and Delphi. This supplier bracket already produces most car components and even manufactures entire vehicles for OEMs today.

Brands

With the shift from individual to shared ownership, the passenger will have a primary relationship with the TaaS provider (who by default we see as the platform owner), not with the OEM. We therefore see the brand value in road passenger transportation residing with TaaS providers, not OEMs.

The future of incumbent car manufacturers

We expect to see four overall strategies available to car manufacturers:

‣ Focus on hardware manufacturing and assembling. The TaaS vehicle assembly market will be a high-volume, low-margin business. As companies like NVIDIA and Google's Waymo provide the computing platforms and vehicle operating systems for AVs, we would expect to see more companies entering the vehicle hardware market. Incumbent OEM manufacturers will be competing with existing automotive suppliers (e.g., Delphi, Continental, Magna) as well as new entrants including electronics assemblers (e.g., Foxconn), electric vehicle companies (e.g., BYD, NIO) and electric bus companies (e.g., Proterra). More companies will be competing for a market where fewer vehicles are needed.

‣ Build and operate fleets for TaaS providers. This business model would require carmakers to not only manufacture vehicles but also to operate and maintain them throughout their lifecycle. The emphasis of this business would be on providing vehicles at the lowest possible cost-per-mile for the longest possible lifetime. It would be a radical departure from the conventional OEM strategy of "pushing steel." The new business model would reward companies that build vehicles with long lifetimes and the lowest possible lifetime cost of ownership. Making a transition to this dramatically different business model would then be a matter of cultural and organizational management.

‣ Forward integrate to become a TaaS platform provider. The manufacturing and fleet operations businesses will be commodity businesses. The relationship with the passenger, as well as the brand value and profit potential, will shift to the TaaS platform provider. Companies like GM, BMW and Ford have started to realize this and have been investing in building capabilities to address these market opportunities. OEMs face a set of challenges because of a range of factors including: i) TaaS platforms require a particular skill set and culture and require the product-development speed of Silicon Valley high-tech software companies, not Detroit hardware companies; ii) the pressure to preserve OEM cash flows and sunk costs by pushing uncompetitive ICE vehicles; and iii) the likelihood that network effects will lead to the survival of a small number of platforms in any given geographical area.Vertical Integration. Car manufacturers may aim to be vertically integrated providers of A-EVs and TaaS service, participating in all parts of the value chain, including manufacturing, fleet operations, TaaS platform and vehicle operating system development. Some OEMs have invested in creating capabilities to make this possible. Ford and GM have acquired Silicon Valley self-driving technology companies, while Nissan has chosen to develop its own self-driving capability in-house.

Tactics that car manufacturers that survive are likely to employ in advance of the disruption point include:

‣ Ramping up EV/AV vehicle manufacturing capacity before 2020 to ensure supply of vehicles is available in the early market-grab dynamic of the early TaaS rollout.

‣ Acquiring companies building AV software.

‣ Focusing on driving down vehicles' cost-per-mile, lowering operating costs and increasing lifetime.

‣ Stopping capital expenditures and R&D spending on individually owned vehicles and focusing on developing TaaS vehicles, including modularizing vehicle architecture, for ease of assembly, for different sizes of vehicle, and for ease of maintenance. Designing for high mileage utilization and end of life.

‣ Partnering with or developing alternative revenue streams — such as advertising and entertainment — to help drive down net cost-per-mile.

‣ Partnering with, acquiring or creating TaaS platforms.

‣ Being at the forefront of AV trials and pilots globally.

‣ When AVs are approved, flooding urban markets with vehicles to seize market share.

‣ Leading the "roll-up" of local platform operators.

‣ Using existing relationship with car owners to radiate outwards from urban centers to suburban and rural areas.

» 2.3 The Disruption of Oil

The TaaS disruption poses existential threats to the oil industry. Our findings indicate that global oil demand will peak around 2020 at about 100 million barrels per day, falling to about 70 mbpd by 2030 (see Figure 11). The effects of such a dramatic decrease will ripple through the whole value chain, causing systemic disruption from oil fields to pipelines to refineries.

We find that the implications of the TaaS disruption on the oil industry have not been fully recognized by the market. Current valuations of listed oil companies imply that stockholders are still basing their spreadsheet scenarios on the continuation of the individual ownership model, forecasting growth in revenues and cash flow for decades to come.

This section looks at the implications of the disruption of oil.

Rethinking oil demand under TaaS

Methodology

We modeled oil demand for the TaaS disruption, based on the following key assumptions:

- ‣ U.S. passenger vehicle oil demand. We calculated the displaced oil demand from U.S. light-duty vehicle transport corresponding to the adoption rate forecast in Part 1.

- ‣ Disruption of Trucking. We then included a 5% annual change in oil demand from 2021 from the disruption of medium and heavy-duty vehicles in the U.S.

- ‣ Extrapolation of U.S. data globally. We then extrapolated these U.S. trends to Europe and China in the same year, and to the rest of the world with a four-year time lag, in order to approximate the disruption to global oil demand.

- ‣ Business as usual (BAU) for remaining oil demand. For all other sources of oil demand in transport and other sectors, we assume BAU according to EIA forecast scenarios. We do not account for disruption to oil demand elsewhere in the transport sector, such as in aviation or shipping.

U.S. oil demand from passenger road transport drops by 90% by 2030

Using the EIA's BAU forecasts as the baseline, the results of our analysis indicate that oil consumption from U.S. passenger vehicles will decline from over 8 million bpd in 2020 to under 1 million bpd in 2030. Over 7 million bpd of oil demand will be eliminated by the TaaS disruption. The implication is that around 90% of the U.S. passenger vehicle market demand for oil will evaporate within a decade.

Figure 10. Oil demand in U.S. light-duty vehicle

Source: BAU based on EIA figures

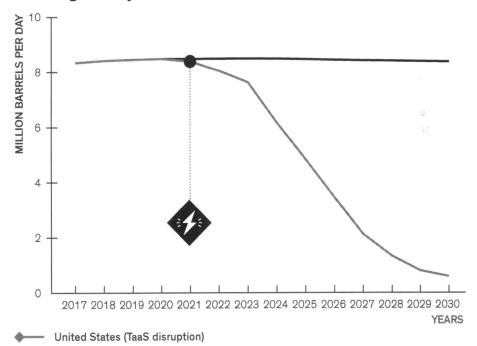

» U.S. light-duty vehicle oil-demand forecast

United States (TaaS disruption)
United States (BAU)

Oil demand from trucking drops by 7 million bpd globally

Similar dynamics that enable the disruption of passenger vehicle transport also apply to the trucking industry, where we see A-EV trucks enabling a quick shift to TaaS.[65]

Labor and fuel are about 69% of operating costs of a truck in the U.S.[66] and 71% in China.[67] By replacing the human driver and bringing an order-of-magnitude decrease in the costs of maintenance and fuel, A-EV trucks will incur a substantially lower cost-per-mile. Companies in industries such as logistics that use fleets of trucks will face competitive pressure to lower the cost of shipping by moving to A-EV trucks. The trucking industry has already invested heavily to increase fleet asset utilization to about 50% today.[68] A-EVs will likely increase this percentage. A key enabler will be the fact that autonomous trucks will have no regulatory restriction on the hours they can operate each day, unlike human truck drivers who are legally mandated not to exceed an hours-per-day limit. As with passenger vehicles, an increase in asset utilization triggers substantially lower costs-per-mile over the lifetime of the truck. As a result, company optimization of truck utilization will be critical for commercial survival.

Both incumbent and startup companies have already demonstrated autonomous truck technologies. For example, Daimler has been publicly driving its semi-autonomous truck in Nevada since 2015.[69] However, disruptions usually come from outside the incumbent players. Otto, a startup company founded by an engineer who led the development of Google's self-driving car (now Waymo), was acquired by Uber in 2016.[70]

We do not see range as a constraint in the disruption of ICE trucks. The U.S. Department of Transportation estimates that more than half the freight (by weight) in the U.S. is driven less than 100 miles, while 71% travels less than 250 miles.[71,72] These ranges are within current capabilities — and will continue to improve exponentially over the next decade.[73]

Medium- or heavy-duty vehicles account for 15% of petroleum consumption in the U.S.[74] With a 50% decrease projected between 2020-2030, demand from the A-EV equivalents of these vehicles will decrease from 3 million bpd to less than 2 million bpd in the U.S., with global trucking demand for oil dropping by 5.6 million bpd against the EIA BAU forecasts.[75]

Global oil demand peaks in 2020 at 100 million bpd and plunges to around 70 million bpd by 2030

For our global oil demand scenario, we applied the annual rate of change in light-, medium- and heavy-duty transport oil demand in the U.S. to the oil demand forecasts in China and Europe in the same year, and to the rest of the world with a four-year delay. Figure 11 shows the outcome of this analysis: global oil demand will drop from 100 million bpd in 2020 to 70 million bpd in 2030. That is, total global oil demand will decrease by about 30% in a decade.

Implications for oil producers

We predict three key components of disruption along the oil value chain:

›   **Price collapse.** Low oil prices of $25.4 per barrel (bbl) by 2030 will affect the entire supply chain, but most importantly will drive out expensive producers from the upstream sector. Infrastructure built to service high-cost specific fields will also bear the brunt of lower revenue from oil production.

›   **Volume collapse.** The impact of lower oil demand will be disproportional along the oil supply chain. Certain high-cost countries, companies, and fields will see their oil production entirely wiped out in this demand scenario.

Composition disruption. The dramatic changes in the composition of the demand for refined petroleum products will be another disruptive factor in the oil supply chain. On average, a U.S. refinery produces 19 gallons of gasoline, 10 to 12 gallons of diesel and 4 gallons of jet fuel from each 42 gallon barrel.[76, 77] That is, about 69% of each oil barrel goes to gasoline and diesel. As 30 million barrels per day of gasoline and diesel demand are removed from global markets, the effect on crude oil production might be more profound and disproportional along the oil value chain. This is because oil markets are complex and simple averages do not necessarily apply. There are more than 150 different types of oil crudes processed by more than 600 refineries around the world.[78] These refineries vary widely in their complexity and ability to adapt to shifting changes in oil supply and fuel demand composition. As demand for gasoline and diesel drops many refineries will not be able to adapt to new market conditions by shifting production to other oil 'by-products' such as jet

Figure 11. Global oil demand with TaaS disruption of transport

Source: Authors' calculations using U.S. Energy Information Administration oil demand forecast as a baseline

---

» *Global oil-demand forecast*

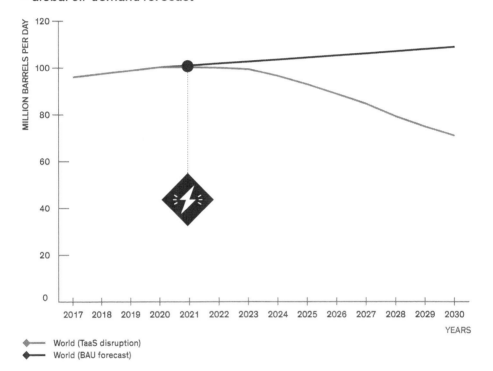

fuel, heating oil, asphalt, petrochemicals and kerosene. They will shut down or face massive investment needs to retrofit to new market realities. A new refinery might take 5-7 years to commission and cost $18 billion[79] while retrofitting an existing refinery might take $3 billion dollars.[80] This means that until the market stabilizes, the 30 mbpd drop in demand of gasoline and diesel (which represent 69% of the output of an oil barrel) may disrupt the value chains of up to 43 mbpd of oil production.

Figure 12. Cash cost of producing a barrel of oil in 2030

Source: Rystad Energy UCube

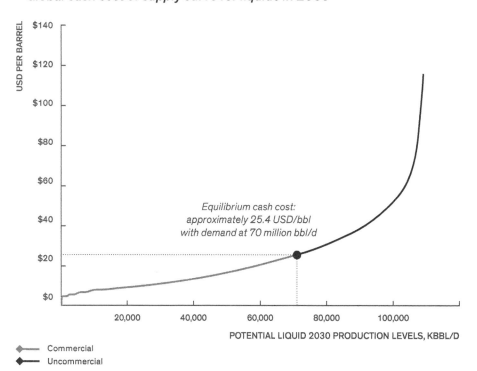

» *Global cash cost of supply curve for liquids in 2030*

Equilibrium cash cost: approximately 25.4 USD/bbl with demand at 70 million bbl/d

Commercial
Uncommercial

Copyright © 2017 **RethinkX**

Oil drops to $25 per barrel or below

Figure 12 shows the equilibrium cash cost[81] of oil in 2030 based on our demand scenario, and analysis and data obtained from Rystad Energy. Assuming demand drops to 70 million bpd by 2030, the market would reach equilibrium at a cash cost of $25.4 /bbl.

Economics dictate that when oil demand drops to 70 million bpd in a competitive market, the 70 million cheapest barrels will be produced. In our model, those barrels that are more expensive than the 70-millionth-cheapest barrel to produce globally will be uncommercial and have no market value. The implication is that high-cost oil will be left in the ground, while the assets associated with extracting this type of oil and the infrastructure (pipelines, refineries) that depends on it will be stranded and valueless.

Short term volatility in oil prices

While it is not our purpose to forecast oil prices in this sector report, we can speculate on how the disruption of transportation might impact prices in the interim. Short-term, prior to oil demand peaking in 2020, it is possible that we will see high volatility and even spikes in oil prices. There is great uncertainty on how shorter-term pricing will play out, but if TaaS builds toward the disruption point in the coming years, and if companies and investors become aware of the momentum, then we might see investment in exploration, production, shipping, refineries and infrastructure begin to dry up. This could lead to bottlenecks in global oil markets that create short-term supply constraints and oil price spikes before the disruption gets underway. Another potential spike would be possible if oil producers collectively decide to maximize short-term cash flow in anticipation of the disruption. This would be possible by temporarily agreeing to withhold just about two million barrels per day from the market.[82]

During the oil crisis of 2014 and 2015, crude oil prices crashed from $115 a barrel in mid-2014 to less than $30 in the beginning of 2015. This happened when supply outstripped demand by two million bpd.[83, 84, 85] Our oil scenario predicts a drop of 30 mbpd by 2030 (which is 40 mbpd below the BAU estimate).

It is also possible that in the short term, prices over-correct as some countries or companies continue to pump oil that is unprofitable in the expectation of a recovery in demand or a future increase in price. National oil companies might continue to make uneconomic investments that in the short term depress prices below the cash cost.[86]

While price volatility will likely rule the short- and medium-term, we are more confident in the long-term implications for oil prices, with a longer-term reversion around the cost of the marginal barrel of oil.

Oil volume collapse

Impact on countries

Figure 13 shows the volume of oil that will be uncommercial under our transportation disruption model across the top 20 countries in the world in terms of potential oil production in 2030. U.S. producers will be hit the hardest by the volume effect, as almost 15 million bpd of US oil — or 58% — will become uncommercial to produce at $25.4 cash cost. Likewise, more than half of oil production in Canada, Brazil, Mexico, Angola and the U.K. will be stranded. In contrast, Persian Gulf countries will be barely affected by shrinking volumes, as 95% or more of the oil in these countries will remain commercially viable.[87] Compared to today, global oil production will be more concentrated in Russia and the Gulf countries by 2030.

Our analysis indicates that countries will be affected disproportionately by the disruption of transportation. The magnitude of the impact on individual countries depends on three main factors:

‣ Volume collapse — the proportion of oil stranded (Figure 13)

‣ Price collapse — the impact of market price (Figure 12) on economically viable oil

‣ The relative importance of oil to the economy (Figure 14)

Rent from oil production is less than 1% of GDP in the U.S., compared to around 40% in Saudi Arabia and Iraq, and around 20% in Iran, Qatar and the U.A.E.

Saudi Arabia, Russia, Iraq and other countries with low cash cost of production will maintain relatively high production levels, but nevertheless will suffer from low oil prices, which will drive down revenues and profit margins from oil. Given that rents from oil are high in these countries, the price collapse will have a significant impact on their government spending and economic growth. Thus, in one way or another, all these oil-producing countries will be heavily affected by the disruption.

Figure 13. Top 20 countries by potential 2030 oil production, split by commercial viability

Source: Rystad Energy UCube

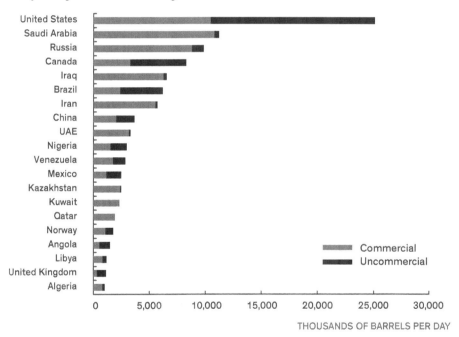

» *Top 20 countries for potential 2030 liquids production, split by commerciality*

THOUSANDS OF BARRELS PER DAY

Copyright © 2017 **RethinkX**

Figure 14. Oil rent as a % of GDP

Source: World Bank World Development Indicators,[88] accessed on 25/01/2017

» Global oil rent in 2014

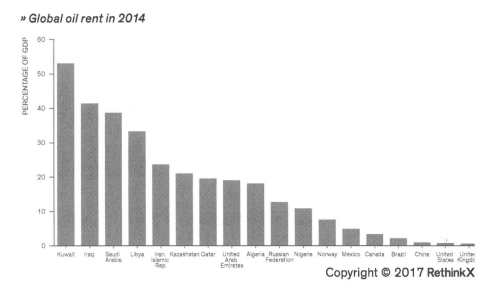

Copyright © 2017 **RethinkX**

Impact on individual oil companies: Large oil companies with high proportion of stranded assets

Our analysis indicates that oil companies will be affected disproportionately by the disruption of transportation. The magnitude of the impact on individual companies depends on two main factors: price and volume.

That is, while global oil demand is forecasted to drop by 30%, companies such as Saudi Aramco would see the rate of uncommercial assets in their portfolio rising to just 4%, and, for companies like Rosneft, approaching 10% (Figure 15).

The picture would be very different for major oil companies such as ExxonMobil, Shell and BP. Assuming that these companies continue to invest under BAU assumptions, they could see 40-50% of their assets become stranded. Furthermore, even the 50-60% of assets that are potentially commercial would still suffer from a market of persistently low prices, causing revenues and earnings to plummet disproportionately.

Figure 15. Potential 2030 oil production for select top companies, split by commercial viability

Source: Rystad Energy UCube

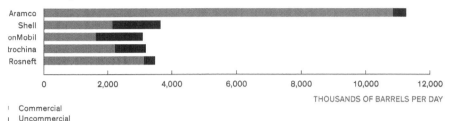

Potential 2030 liquids production for selected top companies, split by commerciality

Impact on oil fields: High-cost oil fields will be stranded

The extent to which countries will be affected by the volume disruption depends on the type of oil fields they have. Persian Gulf countries such as Saudi Arabia, whose production mainly derives from low-cost conventional fields, would barely feel any impact in terms of decreased volume. Countries with a larger share of shale oil, oil sands and offshore oil will see a higher proportion of uncommercial oil. Under a mainstream business-as-usual scenario, shale oil and tight oil could potentially constitute over 70% of U.S. supply in 2030. However, under our transport disruption model, 65% of these barrels would not be commercially viable. Other areas facing large-scale volume disruption include offshore sites in the North Sea (U.K.), Nigeria and Norway; Venezuelan heavy crude oil; Canadian tar sands; and the U.S. shale sites.

Impact on infrastructure: Pipelines and refineries

Infrastructure associated with fields that are largely uncommercial will be heavily impacted. Some key insights include:

‣ The Dakota Access Pipeline (DAPL) would be stranded,[89] as 70% of potential Bakken shale oil becomes uncommercial, leading to excess pipeline capacity. Plans call for the DAPL — a 1,173-mile pipeline designed by Energy Transfer Partners — to carry 470,000 bpd a day.[90] Under our model, existing pipeline capacity will be enough to serve

Bakken, even without the DAPL.

‣ The Keystone XL Pipeline would be stranded,[91] as costly projects will be stranded in the Canadian tar sands. The Keystone XL is designed by TransCanada to carry Canadian tar sands to the Gulf of Mexico for processing at refineries there and export to the international oil markets.[92] Under our model, both the Keystone XL Pipeline and oil sand refineries in Gulf of Mexico will be financially unviable.

‣ Refineries associated with uncommercial fields would need expensive retrofitting or would be shut. Refineries are generally set up to process oil of a particular variety, and different types of crude require different processing methods. Those refineries associated with or located near fields that will become stranded will face severe difficulties, either being forced to close or requiring substantial re-engineering.[93]

Figure 16. Potential 2030 cumulative liquids production, split by supply segment and commerciality

Source: Rystad Energy UCube

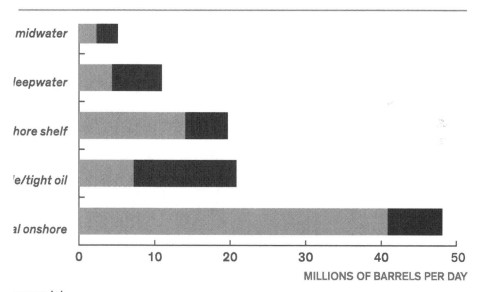

MILLIONS OF BARRELS PER DAY

mmercial
commercial

Box 11: Oil field example

Case study: Bakken Oil Field

Approximately 70% of the potential 2030 production of Bakken shale oil would be stranded under a 70 million bpd demand assumption. Our findings suggest that Exxon Mobil and Apache's Bakken fields will no longer be viable (Figure 17), whereas other larger producers such as Continental Resources and Statoil will see erosion of 60% and 25% of their assets, respectively.

Figure 17. Top 20 Bakken producers listed by potential 2030 oil production, split by commercial viability

Source: Rystad Energy UCube

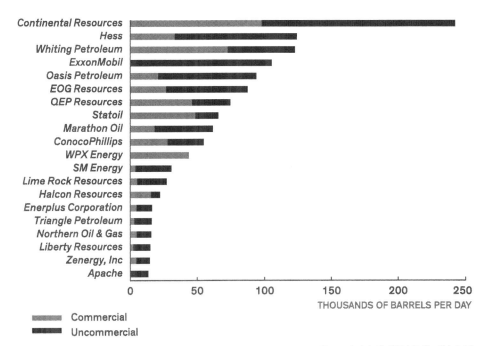

» Top 20 Bakken producers for potential 2030 liquids production, split by commerciality

Commercial
Uncommercial

Copyright © 2017 RethinkX

Impacts elsewhere in the oil value chain

Specialist engineering/oil services companies

High-cost oil is generally harder to extract and requires more involvement from oil services companies[94] with expertise and focus in this field.[95] These companies might have a disproportionately large exposure to high-cost projects that will be stranded by the demand disruption.

Shipping industry

Oil shipping will certainly be impacted by the volume decline in oil production, and this will lead to an oversupply of tankers and a sharp fall in freight prices. In turn, this could trigger a decline in the demand for new oil tankers, leading to a negative ripple effect along the shipping-construction value chain.

What to expect from oil companies?

Oil companies, as well as companies throughout the oil supply chain, have little room to maneuver as oil demand drops, with few strategies open to them given the speed of the disruption.

The history of disruptions and the specific actions of oil companies suggest that self-disruption or a change of business focus will, in most cases, not be a realistic option. Financial strategy suggests that asset sales or the sale of the whole business would be the optimal way to realize value. Finding a buyer would, of course, get more difficult during a market downturn, just like selling a house after the real estate bubble had burst during the Great Recession.

When denial turns to acceptance, oil companies will attempt to maximize value in multiple ways. Our analysis suggests that we will see an increasing number of companies choosing the following options:

› Selling high-cost assets. These assets might include oilfields, refineries, petrochemical units and pipelines. In response to a changing business landscape and low oil prices, Shell has already pledged to sell $30 billion of oil and gas assets between 2016 and 2018.[96] In early 2017, the company disposed of half of its North Sea oil and gas assets, offshore gas fields in Thailand, and Canadian oil sands projects.[97,98]

- Selling the company. It is possible that, before the markets appreciate the scale of disruption, some oil companies could sell themselves and so maximize value. For instance, Saudi Aramco may raise $100 billion and value the company at $2 trillion, which would make it the biggest IPO in history.[99] Selling or listing a company to "take the money off the table" is a time-limited opportunity and would only help "universal holders" if the sale was to a private or government entity. Sale to another public company would still leave universal holders exposed to the business.

- Split their businesses into oil-based assets and other assets (chemicals, plastics, gas) to protect the "good" business from the problems and liabilities in the "bad" business.[100] This has already happened in the electric utility industry, as companies such as RWE and EON split into disrupted fossil and nuclear "bad companies" and "good" growth-oriented clean-energy companies.

- If they find themselves unable to sell oil assets, then they will likely focus on maximizing cash flow by winding down the business. They will write off or write down high-cost assets, cut capital expenditure and overhead, and offload as many liabilities as possible, preferably to unsuspecting taxpayers (see below). Exxon conceded that it may have to write down as many as 4.6 billion barrels in North American reserves in what would be the "biggest accounting reserve revision" in its history.[101]

- Fight through government action and regulatory capture. Focusing on policy, regulation and subsidy to slow down or create barriers to AV and EV technologies, the key enablers of TaaS. Look for the revolving door between governments and the oil industry to go into high gear. Additionally, the oil industry will invest in influencing the public opinion against the adoption of autonomous technologies. In an era of post-truth politics, we expect a steady stream of falsehoods, fake news, FUD (fear, uncertainty and doubt) news and pseudoscience, to be produced in an attempt to shape public perceptions of AV technologies.

Liabilities in wind-down scenario

Investors, employees and taxpayers should be aware of the potential pitfalls of this strategy, and will need to fully understand the potential liabilities of oil companies, including contingent liabilities in assessing value to be realized here. Value destruction can happen in advance of a collapse in volume. The coal sector has seen almost total market-value destruction as coal volumes peaked and dipped only slightly, an effect exacerbated by their liability profile.

Liabilities to be aware of include the potential claim on cash flows of:

‣ Debt holders

‣ Workers — pension liabilities, healthcare liabilities and redundancy costs

‣ Guarantees to other group entities

‣ Lease payment obligations

‣ Take or pay obligations

‣ Clean-up costs — decommissioning, removal and restoration of wells and other facilities

» Part 3:
Implications.
Planning for the Future
of Transportation

» Summary

In Part 3 we explore the social, economic, environmental and geopolitical implications of the TaaS disruption. We look at the likely impacts within road transport systems, signposting both the benefits and negative impacts for countries, businesses, consumers and communities.

Key findings

› **U.S. household disposable income boost.** Savings to consumers from adoption of TaaS could increase aggregate U.S. household disposable income by $1 trillion annually by 2030.

› **Increased GDP.** Due to productivity gains of $1 trillion.

› **Oil disruption.** Lower volumes and prices of oil will have geopolitical implications for energy security, military spending and regional stability.

› **Environmental, health and social benefits.** The new TaaS-based road passenger transport system will reduce CO_2 emissions, lower air pollution, improve health, increase the efficiency of material use, significantly enhance mobility and significantly reduce social inequality due to lack of access to transportation.

› **CO_2 emissions reductions.** TaaS vehicles have an order-of-magnitude lower lifetime CO_2 emissions as compared to IO ICEs.

› **Driving jobs.** Will be lost as a result of TaaS, resulting in aggregate income losses of up to $200 billion.

› **New industry.** The creation of the multi-trillion-dollar TaaS industry will create wealth comparable to or larger than that generated by the personal computer, internet or mobile telephony booms.

Policy recommendations

There are several policy pathways that can assist the development of TaaS in ways that optimize the benefits and mitigate the adverse consequences, including:

▸ Permitting the testing and adoption of A-EVs.

▸ Establishing industry standards for passenger-data ownership and privacy as well as vehicle network security.

▸ Launching open-data initiatives to make municipal road and traffic information available to the public and entrepreneurs.

▸ Encouraging open-access technology development ecosystems, whereby entrepreneurs worldwide can develop and access open-source software and hardware, open data, open mapping, open AI and open education to develop TaaS platforms, AVs and EVs. These initiatives can help lower barriers to developing TaaS products and entering the TaaS market. This can in turn keep larger TaaS providers from exerting monopoly pricing power and ensure that benefits from lower costs-per-mile are passed on to consumers in all markets.

▸ Developing planning strategies for the reuse of unneeded transport infrastructure, parking lots and roadside parking spaces.

▸ Easing regulatory frameworks for the conversion of unneeded commercial garages to social and productive uses such as affordable housing, co-working spaces, art studios, in-law units, student housing and walk-up spaces.

▸ Anticipating and legislating mitigation of negative impacts, including providing social, financial and health care safety nets, as well as re-training programs for displaced workers including (but not limited to) drivers and workers in disrupted oil and ICE sectors.

▸ Investing in public education campaigns to communicate the financial, social, health and environmental benefits of TaaS and to foster public acceptance and trust.

» 3.1 Introduction

TaaS is likely to trigger a global competition to lead the disruption of the road transport system. Even without TaaS, technology companies, battery manufacturers and other key players in the A-EV race are motivated by a range of economic and social incentives. Policymakers in the U.S. and elsewhere have already started to devise smart policies to facilitate the transition to new mobility systems.[102]

Understanding the potential impacts of commercialized A-EVs and the resulting adoption of TaaS on road transport and the broader economy, as well as its economic, environmental and social implications, is a critical precursor to the development of enabling legislation and mitigation policies.[103] See Figure 18 for a summary of the main potential impacts of A-EVs and TaaS.

There are many broader potential implications of this disruption across society. In this section, we highlight the social and economic implications, the environmental implications and the geopolitical implications. We also consider the toolbox available to policymakers.

Choices for policymakers

Policymakers will face multiple moments when their decisions will either accelerate or slow down the transition to TaaS. They could either enable leadership of technology innovation and accelerate the speed of transition or resist the disruption and lock into a high-cost transport infrastructure.

›   **Leaders of disruption** will benefit from positive impacts of new transport systems, devise enabling legislation, plan for new infrastructure and mitigate the adverse impacts.

›   **Resisters of disruption** will treat potential negative impacts as reasons for opposing TaaS, continue investing in high-cost infrastructure, and lobby against adoption of A-EVs and TaaS.

Figure 18. Potential Impacts of TaaS

» *Potential impacts*

POSITIVE IMPACTS

Significant consumer savings and productivity gains
Increased mobility and accessibility for those who cannot drive
Fewer road accidents, fatalities and hospitalizations due to human error
Lighter and less material-intensive vehicles
Improved air quality and public health
Decoupling of energy and geopolitics
Potentially less military spending overseas
Lower infrastructure costs
Less traffic congestion
Reclaiming parking spaces and infrastructure for productive uses
Lower CO_2 emissions

NEGATIVE IMPACTS

Formation of oligopolies/monopolies among TaaS providers
Job losses
Shrinking of government revenues from oil and parking

» 3.2 Social and Economic Implications

Total U.S. household disposable income could increase by $1 trillion annually by 2030

Accessing TaaS will have significant savings[104] for U.S. households. Our model estimates that cost reductions in personal transport across the U.S. will increase household disposable income by over $1 trillion (see Figure 7). The average American family spends $9,000 of its income on road transport every year. Switching to TaaS would result in yearly savings of around $5,600 per household.

The disruption is likely to have large impacts on the broader economy. On one hand, the increase in households' disposable income will boost spending, with positive impacts on job growth across the economy. On the other, TaaS will reduce the number of jobs in the disrupted sectors.

Time freed from driving could increase GDP by an additional $1 trillion dollars by 2030

Americans spend roughly 140 billion hours in vehicles every year. The average vehicle has 1.5 passengers, so the time spent driving is 87 billion hours. If Americans were freed from driving to work or study, they could increase U.S. GDP by $0.5 trillion to $2.3 trillion by 2030.[105] For context, the U.S. had a GDP of $18.56 trillion in 2016. The GDP benefits would accrue to the U.S. as a whole, not just the transportation sector. This potential contribution to U.S. GDP would likely act as a spur for policymakers to support TaaS adoption. The key point is that TaaS has the potential to trigger a significant productivity gain. The calculations above are indicative; their value lies in signposting the self-evident productivity gains that TaaS could bring to the American economy.

Job losses from driving will reduce income by $200 billion, but new jobs will emerge

Driving jobs will be stranded by autonomous technologies. The U.S. auto industry employs 1.25 million directly and 7.25 million indirectly.[106] Five million jobs nationwide could potentially be lost due to self-driving vehicles[107] (including 3.5 million truck drivers[108,109]), equating to 3% of the U.S. workforce. At the same time, new jobs will emerge in a shared mobility transport system serviced by electric and self-driving vehicles.[110] If we assume that a net 5 million driving jobs are lost at an annual average salary of $40,000,[111] this would equate to a reduction in income nationally of $200 billion.

Policymakers will need to anticipate and mitigate the negative impacts of job losses, including providing social, financial and healthcare safety nets as well as re-training programs for displaced workers, including (but not limited to) drivers and workers in disrupted oil and ICE sectors. (This will be the subject of a future RethinkX paper).

Increases in mobility and accessibility

Mobility improvements

Providing mobility and accessibility for all is an important function of the transport system. The availability of on-demand door-to-door transport[112] via TaaS vehicles will improve the mobility of those who are unable to drive and those who cannot currently afford to own cars, including populations living on fixed or highly variable incomes. This impact is particularly significant in the U.S., where a large share of the population relies on driving due to urban sprawl and the low density of public transport infrastructure.

Improved access to workplaces and public services

TaaS will have the benefits of better connectivity and reduced travel time compared to public transport,[113] along with lower costs compared to driving private vehicles. In the U.S., where the average proximity of residents to the nearest public transport stop is lower than in Europe, TaaS will likely reduce travel times even more. Faster and cheaper commutes will help to ensure that access to job opportunities, health and education services are available to all.[114]

» 3.3 Environmental Implications

There will be positive local and global environmental benefits arising from TaaS, but there could also be negative outcomes. We highlight the key issues below.

CO_2 emissions reductions from light-duty vehicles will fall by 90%

One of the primary environmental benefits of switching to an electric, autonomous and shared personal transport system is the reduction of CO2 emissions. The transport sector contributes 26% of CO_2 emissions in the U.S.,[115] of which two-thirds comes from light-duty vehicle fuel combustion.[116, 117] The new transport system would support U.S. climate commitments. [118] Our model shows that the TaaS disruption would trigger a reduction of over 90% in CO_2 emissions from light-duty vehicle road transportation in 2030, compared to BAU projections.[119]

Electricity demand in the U.S. will increase by 18% compared to BAU

Charging A-EVs will increase electricity demand. Our estimates show that the A-EV fleet required under TaaS will use 733 billion kWh of electricity per year in 2030. This represents an 18% increase in total electricity demand in the U.S. in 2030,[120] compared to the business-as-usual projections of the U.S. EIA (see Figure 19). While A-EVs will account for a relatively small share of electricity demand in the U.S., three quarters of growth in electricity demand will come from the expanding A-EV fleet. It is important to note that the increase in demand (kWh) does not imply a need to increase the capacity (kW) of the existing infrastructure. This is because the existing power system is built for peak demand, not efficiency. By scheduling A-EV charging in off-peak periods, we believe that the existing infrastructure can absorb an 18% increase in demand without material investments in generation infrastructure.

Energy demand for transportation in the U.S. will decrease by 80% compared to BAU

The TaaS fleet would use 2.5 quadrillion BTUs as opposed to 12.9 quadrillion for the BAU case[121] with an ICE fleet. That is, A-EVs will reduce road transportation energy demand by 80%. It is important to note that while electricity demand would increase by 18%, total energy demand will decrease by 80%. This is because A-EVs are far more energy efficient than ICE vehicles. The shift from ICE to A-EVs may represent the single largest reduction in CO_2 emissions in the U.S. A parallel shift to a clean energy grid means that the U.S. will have an essentially emissions-free road transportation system by 2030.

» TaaS as a share of total electricity demand in the U.S.

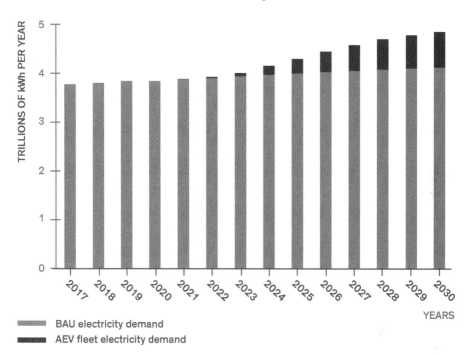

BAU electricity demand
AEV fleet electricity demand

Copyright © 2017 **RethinkX**

Per-mile CO_2 emissions from A-EV production are far lower than ICEs

There is a widespread myth that A-EVs will emit more greenhouse gases during production than ICEs. This is not the case when production emissions are applied on a per-mile basis, across vehicle lifetimes.

The emissions improvement factors for A-EVs are threefold: from production, from tailpipes and from vehicle lifecycle emissions, including those from recycling/disposal.

As noted above, A-EV tailpipe emissions are zero if batteries are powered from renewables. For lifecycles, the emissions savings are around 50%, as borne out in studies of EVs sold in 2015 in the US.[122,123]

In terms of production, A-EVs might appear to have a worse emissions profile: one study found that manufacturing an EV has 15-68% higher emissions than manufacturing an ICE vehicle, mostly due to emissions associated with the production of the lithium-ion battery.[124] Other studies report similar findings. [125,126] However, the comparison is based on several assumptions that require scrutiny:

‣ "Mileage for EVs and ICE will be equal."[127] This assumption does not hold if we compare an A-EV operating under TaaS and an ICE under IO, as an A-EV has a lifetime of 500,000 miles, which is two and a half times that of an ICE. When taking the difference in lifetime mileage into account, emissions from A-EV production are lower on a per-mile basis by 33-54%. By 2030, the lifetime of A-EVs will be one million miles, reducing the per-mile emissions from production even further.

‣ "Energy and resources required to manufacture lithium-ion batteries will remain static." This assumption does not consider the significant cost reductions in the manufacturing of lithium-ion batteries, which have fallen 16% per year during last two decades. Battery producers have been learning how to use fewer resources and less energy to produce a given unit (kWh) of energy storage. Therefore, the energy footprint of the production of A-EV batteries has already improved and will likely continue to improve on an exponential basis.

‣ "Manufacturers will use the same dirty energy inputs to build their batteries." Tesla, which has built the world's largest battery factory, at 35GWh, has announced that it will power its factory with 100% clean energy from solar and wind.[128] So Tesla vehicles clearly don't have the same carbon footprint as other EVs, like those from BYD, which are built using a majority-coal grid. Apple has pledged that all its supply chain will run on 100% renewable energy,[129] and its data centers already run on 100% renewable energy. Should Apple enter the A-EV market, its electric cars would have a near-zero carbon footprint.

When taking all these factors into account, we expect the carbon footprint of TaaS A-EVs to be at least an order of magnitude lower than that of ICE vehicles on a per-mile basis — a number that will continue to improve in the foreseeable future.

The new transport system will improve local air quality and public health

A smaller fleet and more efficient driving due to the adoption of A-EVs will reduce congestion and local pollution from fuel combustion, while an electric fleet would eliminate pollution entirely. Air pollution from exhaust gases has detrimental impacts on human health, an effect that is especially severe in cities. Globally, around three million deaths are due to exposure to outdoor air pollution every year.[130] In OECD countries, outdoor air pollution causes $1.7 trillion annual economic cost from premature death[131] and ill health, while in Europe the cost of premature deaths from air pollution is estimated to be more than 1% of GDP.[132] Half of these losses are attributable to road transport.[133] Thus, shifting to an A-EV fleet and reducing the number of cars on the road will improve citizens' health and well-being.

The new transport system could save up to 1.2 million lives worldwide annually

In 2015, 1.25 million people died from road traffic accidents globally, according to the World Health Organization.[134] Moreover, every year up to 50 million people suffer from non-fatal injuries, which impact quality of life and incur economic costs in the aftermath of a road traffic crash. Autonomous vehicles will be safer than human drivers, leading to a decrease in road traffic accidents.

Materials and resource use from vehicle manufacturing will decrease

Switching to A-EVs will have positive impacts on resource efficiency and material use. The three most salient factors are:

› A reduction in material used in each vehicle. The EV powertrain has far fewer parts than the ICE powertrain: There only about 20 moving parts in the EV powertrain versus more than 2,000 in ICEs'.[135]

› A reduction in materials used as a function of the fall in the number of new vehicles in the fleet.

- A reduction in waste as the incentives for car manufacturer survival changes from unit sales to cost-per-mile. As explained above, survival of car manufacturers will depend on building cars with long lifetimes and low operating costs. This means that they will optimize for minimum waste of resources in building and operating vehicles, including designing vehicle platforms with parts that are interchangeable and recyclable.

Furthermore, as traffic accident rates start to go down materially, we can expect OEMs to use lighter materials, as excess material and features that are based on existing traffic accident rates become redundant (see Part 2).

» 3.4 Geopolitical Implications

Here, we analyze two key geopolitical implications: the impact of reduced oil demand and low oil prices on oil producers, regional stability and the energy security of the U.S.; and the geopolitics of lithium in an A-EV dominated world.

Geopolitics of oil

Net oil exporters will be hit hardest by reduced demand and falling price

Declining oil demand and low prices will create political instabilities in parts of the world that are highly dependent on oil, leading to a shifting balance of power in world politics. Many oil fields will cease production as oil drops in price, while low prices will affect the revenue of countries that continue to produce. Oil-dependent countries will be impacted more than those with diversified economies and large financial reserves. Net importers will benefit from both lower cost imports and less dependence on oil exporters.

The net exporter countries that will potentially be most affected by the disruption include Venezuela, Nigeria, Saudi Arabia and Russia. During recent oil crises, Venezuela and Nigeria underwent significant social and economic stress due to their small financial safety nets.[136] In contrast, the impact of low oil prices on Saudi Arabia's GDP was mitigated by its sizable financial reserves, and Russia was also less impacted, despite budget cuts and deepening recession.

Oil-producing countries face increasing political instability

With a sustained oil market downturn, we foresee that some of these countries will face political instability due to growing debt, cuts in social welfare expenditures and increasing poverty and inequality.[137] Destabilization is likely to be greatest in countries where the most severe oil industry declines are experienced.

Energy security will be a less critical factor in U.S. foreign policy

The TaaS disruption will wipe out more than 8 million barrels per day of U.S. oil demand by 2030. In 2015, the United States was a net importer of 4.7 million bpd (it imported 9.4 million bpd and exported 4.7 million bpd).[138] Oil markets and value chains are global, which means that petroleum exporters may also import petroleum technologies, products and services. This means that there is no such thing as petroleum energy independence until oil demand is reduced to zero. However, while the United States will have a high proportion of stranded oil assets, the country will be mathematically independent of oil imports by 2030. Energy security will be a far less critical component of American foreign policy and military strategy. Political instabilities induced by the collapse of the oil industry may have serious geopolitical implications for the U.S. in the short term. However, the country's foreign policy and military strategy may need to be crafted anew, within a context where U.S. energy security is not one of the country's top strategic geopolitical issues.

Geopolitics of lithium
Supply risks will need to be identified

Currently, EV production and design have certain key resource requirements, including lithium, nickel, cobalt and cadmium. Lithium-ion batteries are by far the most critical input in EVs. Considering booming demand for these materials for manufacturing EVs, identifying risks and instabilities in material supply and mitigation strategies is critical to the future of the industry.

Lithium geopolitics is entirely different from oil geopolitics

Lithium is a material stock and, in the EV industry, is only required to build the battery, while oil is a fuel required to operate an ICE vehicle. Lithium scarcity would only affect new vehicle production. Not having lithium is like not having a new engine; the existing fleet can still operate for years. Oil is essential to operate the existing fleet; thus, oil is a far more critical part of the value chain. Without oil, the existing fleet stops operating almost immediately, as the oil shocks of 1973 and 1979 clearly showed. In the short term, the geopolitics of lithium supply is thus less critical, and not remotely analogous to oil supply.

Lithium-ion battery manufacturing has fewer supply constraints

Like oil reserves, lithium is highly concentrated in few countries.[139, 140] Lithium production is also highly concentrated, with four major producers in control of 85% of supply (Sociedad Quimica y Minera de Chile, FMC Corp, Talison and Albemarle Corporation).[141, 142]

Contrary to what their name might imply, lithium-ion batteries only have 2% lithium by volume.[143] The cost of lithium is not a material part of the cost of a lithium-ion battery: It's about 4% (rising from 2% after recent price spikes in lithium).[144] The cost of lithium-ion batteries has decreased by about 70% recently, even as the spot prices for lithium have more than doubled.[145] Our research indicates that the mineral quantities required for battery demand are achievable if there is sufficient advance planning.[146] Lithium is constrained by the relatively long amount of time needed to open mines and build refinery capacity (3-5 years) rather than by any shortage of the raw material itself.

Lithium-ion batteries can be built with close substitute minerals

There are many types of lithium-ion batteries, using different minerals according to the specific needs of the product. Each type of battery uses different chemistries and materials to achieve different purposes. For instance, smartphone providers may design a battery for fast charging but short longevity, because the smartphone is expected to be replaced within two or three years. Stationary grid storage providers, which store electricity at a home, business or on the grid, may design lithium-ion batteries with longer cycle life (say, 20 or 30 years). A battery for a high-end car that needs "insane" acceleration would be designed for higher voltages, while a city bus that doesn't need the acceleration might use a different chemistry.

Tesla cars use lithium-nickel-cobalt-aluminum-oxide (NCA) batteries, while BYD buses use lithium-iron-phosphate (LiFePO$_4$ also known as LFP) batteries.[147] BYD also uses LFP batteries to power its EVs and hybrid EVs. These vehicles don't need the acceleration of a Tesla Model S, but BYD batteries' warranties are for 30 years, while Tesla's warranty is for eight years.

The main components in the most common form of lithium-ion battery, nickel-manganese-cobalt (NMC), are not lithium but a range of materials including cobalt, manganese and aluminum.[148] In 2015, 41% of the global cobalt demand came from the battery industry.[149] Almost all (94%) of cobalt supply is a by-product of nickel or copper operations, which is principally concentrated in the Democratic Republic of the Congo, a high-conflict country, which accounts for 60% of global supply. New mines opening in the near future will add roughly 35% to the global capacity of 94k tons.[150] Limited production and rising global demand for cobalt resulted in a 50% increase in cobalt prices in 2016.[151] Globally, about 68% of lithium-ion batteries are made with cobalt, while 22% are LFP and 20% are LMO (lithium-manganese -oxide).[152] The latter is mainly used in consumer devices. Cobalt supply risk can be mitigated either by changing the balance of cobalt in the cathode or through the use of lithium-iron-phosphate batteries,[153] which do not require cobalt.

About 80% of China's EV batteries are LFP.[154] Tesla recently announced that the company will prioritize sourcing raw materials from North America for its Gigafactory in Nevada, as well as changing its battery chemistry to mitigate material supply risks.[155]

Lithium mineral supply risks can be mitigated through recycling

Lithium batteries from A-EV retirements can be recycled for new batteries and other secondary uses, such as storage for utilities, homes and businesses.[156] Lithium batteries will still have 80% of their original capacity after retirement from road transport.[157]

» Appendix A,
Appendix B
and Endnotes

» Appendix A

Cost Methodology

Introduction

Cost will be the most important factor affecting economic choice. The scale of the cost differential will be the key determinant of consumers choosing TaaS over IO. This section sets out the basis of our assumptions.

Upfront cost analysis

To model upfront cost for new vehicles (see Figure 20), we use the following methodology:

› **Vehicle types.** Our analysis is based on the largest selling vehicles in each of three categories: small, medium and luxury vehicles. For ICE vehicles these are the Honda Civic, Toyota Camry and Mercedes S-Class. For EVs we use the Nissan Leaf, Chevrolet Bolt and Tesla Model S. These vehicles act as the baselines for our analysis.

› **Adjustments.** For EVs we assume that the vehicle will have a 250-mile range by 2020 by increasing the battery size of current vehicles (if required) and applying estimates of increasing battery power density. The other major adjustment we make for EVs is to apply a battery cost of $200/kWh from 2017.

› **Cost forecasts.** These vehicles become proxies for vehicles in that category. We break vehicles into their major constituent parts and apply cost curves to these until 2030. The cost analysis comes from industry data and discussions with experts.

Figure 20. Upfront cost comparison of electric and gasoline vehicles to 2030

Sources: Authors' calculations, Edmunds, Tony Seba and U.S. Department of Energy

» ICE vs EV upfront costs over time

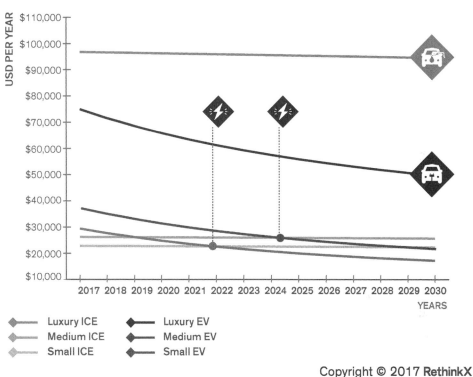

◆— Luxury ICE	◆— Luxury EV	
◆— Medium ICE	◆— Medium EV	
◆— Small ICE	◆— Small EV	

Copyright © 2017 **RethinkX**

For A-EVs in the TaaS fleet, we apply a reduced manufacturing and distribution margin of 8%. This is to account for the commoditization of vehicle production (more akin to electronics assembly), lower brand value and a shorter distribution chain as fleet owners buy direct from OEMs (see Part 2 for further detail).[158]

Depreciation and finance costs

Depreciation for TaaS vehicles (all of which are A-EVs) is calculated as the upfront cost *divided* by lifetime mileage (see below for the basis of this calculation). The upfront cost element is covered in the note above and Figure 20; in this section, we look at vehicle lifetime. As we show, there are several key differences between TaaS and IO vehicle ownership that affect **the treatment of depreciation**, meaning that vehicle lifetime mileage is the critical factor.

Vehicle lifetime

The concept of vehicle lifetime is not black and white; a vehicle reaches the end of its life when it is uneconomic to continue to repair it, with timespans and mileages varying considerably. Longevity can be extended by the replacement of individual parts, but eventually these costs outweigh the costs of buying a new or used vehicle and cease to make economic sense.

Our analysis divides the critical elements of the A-EV four main categories: the drivetrain and battery, the body and interiors, consumables (such as brake pads), and power electronics and sensors.

Our research on these elements analyzed the potential vehicle lifetime and the implications for replacement cycles. All parts are seen as potentially replaceable at the disruption point, and replacement costs are included in our maintenance costs assumptions.

Lifetime analysis

In our analysis we find that the limiting factor is the vehicle battery; we model the end of vehicle life when its battery capacity declines to 80%[159] and attribute no value to an A-EV beyond this point.

However, the write-off assumption is conservative on several fronts. Many parts of the vehicle will, in fact, still have value in other contexts, for example as spares for maintenance in other A-EVs. Additionally, there is likely to be a role for batteries as a component of grid storage,[160] and, longer term, we expect batteries to become replaceable consumables,[161] similar to brake pads.

Higher utilization helps lower cost because some aspects of vehicle degradation are related to time: More miles per period of time lowers the degradation rate of a vehicle and these components, including the battery and the body. The implication is that if still higher utilization (i.e. above 40%) is achieved, this may lower costs-per-mile further.

A key finding is that **A-EVs will last for 500,000 miles by 2021.** This is 2.5 times greater than our estimate for the lifetime miles of an ICE in the same year (200,000). Below, we explain the basis of this assumption.

Powertrain. It is important to note that an A-EV powertrain is much less complex than an ICE; it has 20 moving parts, rather than an ICE's 2,000. Furthermore, it operates in a far more benign environment, in which there is less heat and vibration and fewer touching parts. As a consequence, degradations in A-EVs are much lower, as degradation is mainly caused either by moving parts that touch and degrade each other or by parts that produce heat. The small number of parts also makes EV assembly simple and inexpensive, and they are much more easily replaced than in an ICE. Taken together, these factors make EV technology both intrinsically longer lasting and economically competitive.

Battery. There are numerous chemistries that can be used in lithium-ion batteries, all with different properties that make them more or less useful for different applications. Here we highlight three:

Nickel cobalt aluminum (NCA) or nickel manganese cobalt (NMC): This is the chemistry used by Tesla. It has high specific power, which allows for fast acceleration. High energy density allows for greater range per kg. But this is offset by a shorter lifetime in charge cycles.

Lithium iron phosphate: This is used is buses, trucks and some cars. It is slightly lower cost, and has a longer life in charge cycles. But it has less specific power — less of an ability to accelerate. It has less energy density and hence vehicles get less range per kg.

We assume that larger vehicles that service mainly the TaaS Pool market would be based on lithium iron phosphate or NCA/NMC batteries, and smaller vehicles will rely on NCA/ NMC, though developments in either technology might change the balance. Performance (acceleration) is not a key criterion in a TaaS fleet.

Batteries are degraded by both time and use. In a high-utilization fleet, we do not think that time will cause material degradation to batteries, and so this analysis concentrates on use. The use element of battery lifetime is measured in charge cycles.[162]

Real-life data gathered from 500 Tesla Model S owners who had driven a total of about 12 million miles showed battery degradation of only 5% after 50,000 miles and 8% after 100,000 miles.[163] Tesloop, a California Pre-TaaS startup that uses Tesla Model S and Tesla Model X, has seen battery degradation of just 6% after 200,000 miles. CEO Elon Musk said that Tesla battery simulations showed a degradation of less than 20% after 500,000 miles.

We are confident that lithium iron phosphate batteries are currently capable of 2500-3000[164] charge cycles before they are depleted,[165] and certainly will be by 2021, which we use in our model.[166, 167] With a range of 200 miles, this gives a lifetime of 500,000-600,000 miles. Our model assumes that this increases to 5,000 cycles by 2030, although this is likely conservative.[168]

NCA/NMC batteries are supposed to have shorter lives. However, data from the field suggests these batteries could last significantly longer than predicted.[169] This is preliminary data and cannot be extrapolated from. Below we consider the sensitivity of our cost-per-mile model to battery lifetimes.

We consider 3 different scenarios to look at the sensitivity of our TaaS cost-per-mile figures to battery lifetime. Firstly, where battery life is 500k miles, there would be no battery replacement needed. Secondly, where battery life is 300k miles, it would be replaced once, lifting the vehicle lifetime to 600k miles given that the battery is the limiting factor to lifetime in our model and other parts can last this long. Thirdly, where battery life is 200k miles, the battery would be replaced twice in a 600k-mile lifetime. For a 500k-mile and a 300k-mile battery life, there is no impact on cost-per-mile; the increase in vehicle life to 600k miles offsets the increase in battery costs. For the 200k-mile battery life, there would be an increase of 1 cent per vehicle mile for TaaS. We do not consider that this would materially alter our findings on the speed of adoption.

The battery cycle analysis is based on batteries with a 250-mile range with a depth of discharge of 80%.

Motor. Motors are not new technology, and we have evidence of motor life

---

in other high-utilization environments. EV motors will cover at least 500,000 miles without (or with low) maintenance.[170] Therefore, we do not see motors as a limiting factor within our model.

Vehicle body and interiors. The major impact on vehicle bodies is corrosion. The effects of corrosion are correlated more to time than to mileage, although the latter also plays a role. Environmental conditions also affect corrosion, but it is apparent from decades of ICE vehicle use that A-EV vehicle bodies will extend well beyond 5 years, and even to 9 years as modeled for 2030. The body will not be a limiting factor, with only minor replacements and maintenance required. For interiors, we have looked at replacement cycles for planes, buses and trains as proxies, with only minor costs seen, which we capture in maintenance costs. Durability tests performed on current Proterra electric buses by the Exova Defiance Test Facility showed that after 750,000 miles, "no part of the bus body or other systems were compromised, including the chassis, battery packs and mounting, windows and doors."[171]

Consumables. The repair or replacement of brakes, tires, lights, sensors and other consumables can be easily carried out and are taken into account in the maintenance cost category of our modeling. The current business model for IO vehicles has incentives that drive planned obsolescence and replacement; TaaS incentives will drive the opposite.

For example, the regenerative braking systems used in EV buses and trucks have led to much lower (or no) costs for brake maintenance, one of the most frequently replaced vehicle components within an ICE.[172]

Power electronics and computers. Computer lifecycles tend to be time-based rather than mileage-based and are assumed to be physically robust enough to last for our estimated 5 year/500,000 miles A-EV lifetime. Software is assumed to be kept current through over-the-air updates. This is a different approach from the standard 3-year computer replacement cycle used in depreciation calculations, which favor obsolescence and regular replacement.

Conclusion. Overall, we consider the 500,000-mile lifetime of the vehicle by 2021 to be conservative. Other than the battery, we expect all other parts to last well in excess of 500,000 miles. Our sensitivity analysis around battery lifetime suggests that battery replacement adds little or no cost to TaaS, given the increase in overall vehicle lifetime if the battery is replaced. We also assume that vehicle lifetime will improve at 8% per year, leading to a 1-million-mile lifetime by 2030.

Calculating depreciation

The fall in depreciation costs for an A-EV relative to ICE depreciation costs is the single biggest component of cost savings in the TaaS model when compared to the costs of a new IO ICE. Upfront costs will be recovered in a depreciation charge, part of the cost-per-mile to consumers. There are a number of reasons why the depreciation charge will be different from the treatment of upfront costs in the individual ownership (IO) model (see Box 12). TaaS providers will allocate the upfront cost of the vehicle equally over the lifetime miles of the vehicle.

The calculation will be:

Depreciation = Upfront cost ÷ Expected number of miles in vehicle lifetime

This is entirely different from how depreciation is calculated in the IO model, where depreciation is based on a residual value calculation, which takes the expected drop in value during the period of ownership into account (see Box 12). Given that very few new IO car buyers own a vehicle for its lifetime, lifetime miles play no role in the IO calculation.

Box 12: Calculating depreciation for ICEs and A-EVs

Depreciation of individually owned vehicles (including ICE, EV and AV)

IO vehicles are sold before the end of their economic life. The default assumption for a purchaser of a car is that the vehicle will be sold before the end of its economic life;[173] few owners retain a vehicle for its full lifetime, and many vehicles are leased. We use the lease finance model as the basis for our depreciation analysis, with the standard 3-year lease period as the baseline.

Depreciation of an IO car is a function of the change of vehicle value during ownership. The assumption that ICEs will be sold before the end of their economic lives implies that at the point of sale a vehicle has *residual value*. Depreciation is therefore calculated as the loss in value while the vehicle is owned; that is, the difference between the value at the point of purchase and the residual value.

Vehicle lifetime miles are not used as the basis for IO depreciation. In the IO market, vehicle lifetime miles are not a consideration in cost of ownership. Lifetime miles are not used as the basis for the depreciation calculation; most individual purchasers (and lease finance companies) are primarily interested in how much a vehicle will decline in value over a given period.

Cost-per-mile for IO depreciation is calculated by the decline in value divided by miles driven in the ownership period (in our analysis this is 33,900 miles for a new car, depreciated over 3 years).

Long EV lifetime is not relevant in the IO market. The 500,000-mile lifetime of an A-EV or EV equates to 44 years in the IO market, by which time the vehicle is obsolete. This reinforces our assumption that lifetime miles are not pertinent to depreciation in the IO market.

Depreciation of A-EVs in TaaS fleets

TaaS providers will own an A-EV for its entire lifetime. If they sell them on to each other, the value will be based on the remaining lifetime miles.

Much higher utilization leads to shorter vehicle life in years. We estimate that A-EVs will travel their 500,000 miles in under 5 years.

For accounting purposes, A-EVs are assumed in our model to have no residual value after 5 years. The modeling conservatively assumes that after 5 years (and 500,000 miles) the vehicle will be written off, rather than the constituent parts being re-used.

These factors lead to TaaS depreciation being calculated over the vehicle lifetime on a per-mile basis. As no residual value is expected at the end of the 5-year A-EV lifetime (and no sale during lifetime is expected), then the IO depreciation methodology is not applicable. As a result, we see depreciation of the cost of a TaaS vehicle on a per-mile basis as the logical calculation.

Our assumption is that TaaS providers will attribute upfront cost to lifetime miles evenly.[174] This leads to a huge reduction in the depreciation cost.

The cause for the low depreciation charge per mile in the TaaS model becomes clear: vehicle lifetime — in miles — becomes a key element in the calculation (see Box 12). This is where EV technology has a huge advantage over ICE, with 500,000 lifetime miles by 2021 versus 200,000 for ICEs. In fact, the long vehicle lifetime means that the depreciation cost changes little even if the upfront cost of vehicles improves at a slower rate than we forecast.

The implication for consumers using TaaS is that depreciation will be a small fraction of the cost (1/500,000th of the upfront cost-per-mile). We provide a detailed explanation of why per-mile depreciation costs are lower in TaaS, and why a change in accounting practice can be made, in Box 12.

Finance charges

Finance costs are related to time; higher utilization will see better capital efficiency and lower finance costs on a dollar-per-mile basis. A finance charge is based on an annual or monthly ownership period; because TaaS vehicles will cover 10 times the miles in any period, the cost-per-mile for finance is 10 times less. In our comparative analyses, we treat finance costs for individually owned ICEs generically, irrespective of whether the vehicle is leased or purchased for cash, on the basis that there is an opportunity cost of capital in a cash purchase.

Maintenance costs

Vehicle lifetime, upfront costs and maintenance costs are all closely related. For ICE vehicles there are trade-offs between them: If the product is built robustly, then it will last longer and have lower maintenance costs but the upfront cost will increase. ICEs also have a maintenance cost curve that increases over vehicle lifetime.

These dynamics are different for A-EVs. As discussed above, these vehicles have intrinsically longer lifetimes and lower maintenance costs. Based on our analysis of A-EV maintenance costs over their lifetime, we model costs at 20% of the equivalent ICE vehicle.[175]

This estimate is conservative. Propriety data from high-use bus and truck EVs suggests that on a bottom-up analysis of maintenance costs, a lower figure would be appropriate. Furthermore, "vehicle disruption" could bring down the maintenance costs by modularizing the construction of vehicles with replaceable parts and by eliminating labor costs through automation of the maintenance process. Additionally, consumables can be designed for A-EV lifetimes.

These are significantly different maintenance incentives for ICEs, where the dealership system is highly dependent on a revenue stream from after-sales servicing and maintenance. In contrast, the TaaS industry will use cost-per-mile as its key cost metric. The market will reward companies that achieve the highest possible lifetime mileage at the lowest possible cost. Other companies will simply be unable to compete.

We use two treatments for maintenance in our cost-per-mile analysis for IO ICE vehicles (see Figure 2). For new cars, we take the average maintenance costs for the first 3 years of ownership (to mirror the depreciation treatment). For the existing vehicle stock, when we calculate the operating cost alone of a IO ICE vehicle in Figure 2, we take the lifetime maintenance cost over 200,000 miles and calculate a per-mile average.

Insurance

As in the rest of the TaaS value chain, the insurance market will move to a cost-per-mile basis rather than an annual premium. We estimate a 90% reduction for A-EVs, relative to driver-controlled ICEs. This is based on analysis of the two principal components of insurance costs: 1) theft and 2) liability, injury and vehicle damage.

Theft

Although it would be possible for hackers to remotely steer a vehicle away, the risk of theft by this means will be low. Given that A-EVs will have cameras, GPS, vibration sensors and dozens of positioning sensors, alerting and tracking the vehicle would be done quickly and automatically, and recovering them would be relatively painless. In fact, stolen vehicle recovery success rates of 94% are already being achieved using today's technologies.[176] Whatever theft risks do exist initially will diminish with improvements in digital automotive technology and by developing an effective cyber security strategy.[177] For instance, using encryption, authentication and AI could help detect anomalies that are not part of the auto digital technology and block breaches once a threat is identified.[178] Just as we have seen the evolution of security of computing systems, we might also expect the elimination of the theft component of insurance.

Liability, injury and vehicle damage

Current safety data suggests at least a 90% reduction in the number of accidents involving A-EVs, relative to ICEs.[179] This is because 94% of ICE collisions are related to human error.[180] Additionally, we see the road safety performance of A-EVs improving over time, as AI-based learning improves safety and collisions are virtually eliminated.

In some ways, semi-autonomous vehicles are already safer than human drivers. According to CEO Elon Musk, Tesla's Autopilot feature is already twice as safe as a human driver. According to a 2016 NHTSA report, Tesla crash rates decreased by 40% after it introduced its Autopilot capability in 2015.[181] A 40% yearly improvement rate (slightly slower than Moore's Law) means that AVs will be five times safer than human-driven vehicles by 2020, and 10 times safer by 2022. Moore's Law only measures hardware improvement. The real improvement in AV over the last few years has been in deep learning software. A huge advantage of software is that anything that any vehicle learns, it can upload and share with every other vehicle on that network. If a single Tesla vehicle learns to avoid hitting a cow in Christchurch, New Zealand, it can upload that to the Tesla cloud and share it with every other Tesla vehicle worldwide. Overnight, all Tesla vehicles will know how to avoid hitting a cow. The more Tesla cars on the road, the more learning and sharing happens, and pretty soon a Tesla car in Christchurch will know how to drive in the snow because it learned it from a Tesla in Oslo. In other words, the rate of AV improvement over human drivers will accelerate and achieve near zero collisions much sooner than most experts anticipate.

Our improvement estimates do not include the likelihood of order-of-magnitude technology breakthroughs. For instance, Intel has invested billions of dollars in purchasing companies that will help the company enter the AI technology market. Intel recently predicted that it would deliver a 100× increase in performance in deep learning training.[182] Given enough real-life data, this type of performance improvement would dramatically accelerate the timeline to zero collisions.

However quickly AV improvement over human driving, insurance for TaaS providers will be lower than IO vehicles by an order of magnitude by 2020. Insurance will be based on real-time data, not demographic or geographic actuarial tables. It will be based on cost-per-mile, not on a yearly premium basis. Additionally, vehicles will be owned by fleets that will have bargaining power over insurance companies that individual owners do not have. The insurance market might also be impacted by increasing provision of self-insurance from OEMs, as evidenced by recent announcements from Volvo, Mercedes and Google.[183]

At the same time, human drivers might be faced with increased premiums as the risks of human drivers increases relative to AVs. Human driving may come to be seen as a "reckless" alternative to autonomous driving. As A-EVs improve road safety, the courts could begin to attribute more weight to human error caused by distraction, drunk driving and carelessness.

Fuel costs

We model two major improvements in fuel costs. The first is the improvement in fuel efficiency of EVs over ICE. Powering an EV with electricity is far cheaper than running an ICE on gasoline. Switching to EVs will result in fuel cost savings of 70%. The second improvement is related to driving efficiency when comparing A-EVs and human drivers. Since A-EVs are capable of driving in a more fuel-efficient manner, we allow for a 20% improvement in our model.[184]

Platform and vehicle operating costs

These costs are treated in our modeling as a percent of the total per-mile cost associated with TaaS vehicle fleets. The cost of using a platform (the interface that connects the customer and the management of the A-EV fleet) is treated as 20% of the cost of a passenger mile.[185] We include operating system costs in the upfront cost of the TaaS fleets, at $2500 in 2021. The competitive market environment of the early stages of the TaaS disruption will ensure that price trends toward cost. Given that both the operating system and the platform are essentially software based (with low marginal cost), we see little room in these markets for businesses to charge beyond this level.

Source: Authors' calculations

» New IO ICE vs. TaaS costs

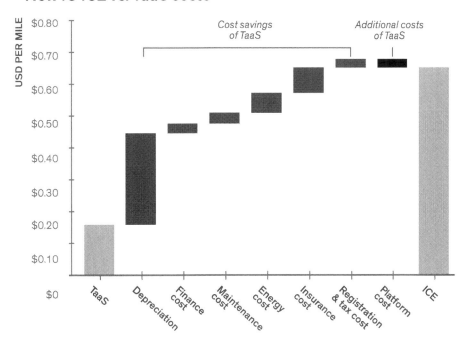

» Appendix B

The Seba Technology Disruption Framework™

RethinkX uses the Seba Technology Disruption Framework™ to help analyze and model the disruptions in this study. Developed by Tony Seba, this framework is the result of more than a dozen years of research and teaching technology disruptions, business model innovation, finance, and strategic marketing of high-tech products and innovations at Stanford Continuing Studies, and has been used to understand and anticipate disruptions in several industries. The framework was the backbone of Seba's 2014 book "Clean Disruption," which has accurately predicted the ongoing disruption of energy and transportation due to technologies such as batteries, electric vehicles, self-driving vehicles and solar PV.

Here is a primer that summarizes the Seba Framework.

Disruption: A disruption happens when new products and services create a new market and, in the process, significantly weaken, transform or destroy existing product categories, markets or industries.

The digital camera disruption destroyed the film camera industry. However, disruption does not always imply the destruction of an existing market. For instance, the web significantly weakened but did not destroy the newspaper publishing industry. Ride hailing has radically transformed the taxi industry, but has not (yet) destroyed it.

Disruptions are made possible by the convergence of technologies and business-model innovations enabled by these technologies. Disruptions are also accelerated by open access technology development.

Convergence: Several technologies, each one improving at a different rate, converge at a certain point in time to make it possible for new products or services to be developed. Apple and Google launched the iPhone and Android products within months of each other in 2007. That's because the convergence of technologies that made the smartphone possible — in terms of bandwidth, digital imaging, touchscreen, computing, data storage, the cloud, lithium-ion batteries and sensors — all happened around 2007. By combining technology cost curves and business model innovations, the Seba Technology Disruption Framework can help anticipate when a given set of technologies will converge and create opportunities for entrepreneurs to create disruptive products and services. For example, Seba's book "Clean Disruption" (2014) accurately predicted that the market would commercialize electric vehicles with 200-mile range at a cost of $35,000 to $40,000 (unsubsidized) by 2018. The GM Bolt and the Tesla Model 3 — leading a wave of such EVs — are now being pre-sold by the hundreds of thousands.

Technology cost curves: Technologies have cost-improvement curves, which show the rate at which a given technology improves over time. The best known technology cost curve is Moore's Law, which postulates that computing power doubles every two years or so. The Seba Framework studies the economic side of these technology-improvement curves; that is, it looks at how a given unit improves on a per-dollar basis. For instance, when analyzing batteries, the metric we may look at is cost in dollars per kilowatt-hour.

For lithium-ion batteries, the cost per kilowatt-hour ($/kWh) improved at a 14% rate between 1995 and 2009.[186] Technology cost curves improve due to a combination of factors, including increased investments, research and development, manufacturing scale, experience and learning effects, openness, competition, standards, ecosystem integration, application across industries and the size of the market(s). Solar photovoltaic, when measured in dollars per watt ($/W) has improved from about $100 per watt in 1970 to about 33 cents per watt in 2017. This is an improvement rate of about 11.4% per year.

When we look at technology cost curves, it's important to know what the main driver of the improvement is. Swanson's Law postulates that solar PV costs tend to fall by about 20% for every doubling of cumulative shipped volume.[187] Therefore, in the case of solar PV, the technology cost curve is mainly driven by volume, not time. Seba predicted in his 2009 book "Solar Trillions" that the cost of unsubsidized solar energy would be as low as 3.5 cents per kilowatt-hour by 2020, thus beating oil, coal, and nuclear. This prediction has recently come true.[188] Demand for both coal and nuclear have peaked and declined, and market values of listed companies in both industries have collapsed as a result.

Exponential Technologies: Technology cost curves and their underlying performance improvement rates vary widely. Information and communication technologies have had high annual improvement rates (Moore's Law has been around 41% per year), while solar PV technology has improved comparatively slowly (11.4% per year). The concept of exponential technologies, coined by Ray Kurzweil, refers to very fast technological change.[189] While he didn't draw a clear line as to what improvement rate makes a technology exponential, his work has emphasized technologies that double their performance every year or two. Moore's Law points to a doubling of computing performance every two years, while wireless communication was improving even faster, doubling performance every 10 to 11 months. The power of exponential technologies is that their performance vastly exceeds the human brain's mostly linear comprehension of growth. For instance, Hendy's Law postulated in 1998 that digital imaging had been improving at about 59% per year (measured as pixels per dollar). A 59% cost curve implies that the technology would improve by about 100 times in ten years, 10,000 times in twenty years, and 1 million times in thirty years. Steve Sasson invented the first digital camera in 1975.[190] If Kodak had applied Hendy's Law to Sasson's invention, it would have predicted that in 2005 a $100 digital camera would perform at a level that would have cost $100 million to achieve in 1975. Kodak's profits peaked in 1999, and the company went bankrupt in 2012.[191] Both Hendy and Sasson worked at Kodak at the time of their discoveries. Other exponential technologies include sensors, artificial intelligence, 3D printing and DNA sequencing.

Technology cost curve improvement rates are not static. Sometimes they slow down temporarily or permanently. For instance, the internal combustion engine, which helped enable the car disruption of horse transportation a century ago, has not materially improved in decades. Small improvements in the cost-to-performance ratio of these technologies may require massive investments. Technology cost curves can also accelerate. Batteries improved by 14% annually for about 15 years. This improvement enabled computer laptop computers, and later, smartphones. From 2010 to 2016, lithium-ion batteries improved by about 20% per year.[192] As the cost per kilowatt-hour of lithium-ion decreases it helps to enable new markets, such as grid storage, residential electricity storage, unmanned aerial vehicles, and robots. The virtuous cycle continues to drive down costs where it can converge with other technologies to help enable disruptions of different markets at different points in the technology cost curve.

Disruption models

The Seba Technology Disruption Framework™ includes four key models that clarify how disruptions take place.

1. **Disruption from below:** *(Clayton Christensen)* A new product or service that is originally inferior compared to what the mainstream market offers improves its performance while decreasing costs at a faster rate than incumbent products.[193] This faster rate of improvement is due to cost curves of the key technologies used to develop the product. This product may initially serve the needs of niche markets, and as it improves its utility, it expands into new markets. Eventually it overtakes and disrupts incumbent products and markets. Examples include personal computers and solar power.

2. **Disruption from above:** *(Tony Seba)* A new product is superior but more expensive than competing products in the mainstream market. In time, however, the cost of the product is lowered until it becomes less expensive than incumbent products. By understanding the technology cost curves of the disrupting product, it is possible to predict when the disruption will take place. It is important to note that many times, these disruptive products are not just one-for-one substitutes, so analysts and industry experts don't understand the coming disruption. The smartphone is a recent example. When the Apple iPhone came out at about $600 in 2007,[194] experts said that it was not disruptive. Who would want to buy a $600 phone when they could buy a $100 Nokia cell phone?[195] What they did not understand is that a smartphone is not just a phone. An iPhone is a platform that allows us to do hundreds of things, including finding a date, getting driving directions, doing online banking, and, yes, making phone calls. The smartphone is not and never was a one-to-one substitute for the conventional cell phone. The electric vehicle (EV) is another example of a disruption from above. The EV is a superior product in a number of ways, not just an electric version of an ICE car.[196] "Clean Disruption" lists nine reasons why the

EV is disruptive. For instance, the battery in an EV allows us to power an average American home for a day or two (and up to two weeks in India).

3. **Big bang disruption:** *(Larry Downes and Paul Nunes)* A new product is better, faster, and cheaper than mainstream products on the day it is launched.[197] Incumbent products have little or no time to react and are quickly disrupted. Examples include Google Maps with driving directions API, which disrupted the then growing GPS market served by companies like Tom Tom and Garmin. The Transportation as a Service (TaaS) disruption highlighted in this report is a Big Bang Disruption.

4. **Architectural disruption:** (Seba) A new product radically changes the way products and services are produced, managed, delivered, and sold. The architecture of the conventional electric power industry is centralized: it generates electricity with a small number of large power plants and delivers the electricity to millions of customers downstream in real time. Solar energy and batteries flip the architecture of electricity: they enable millions of customers to generate, store, manage, and trade electricity. When the cost curves of solar and batteries (plus sensors, power electronics, software, and new business models) converge, the central generation model is disrupted. At that point, the architecture of energy flips from central generation to distributed generation. Architectural disruption is thus not just about technologies disrupting an existing market from below or above. Solar PV (plus storage) is disrupting every form of conventional power generation (coal, nuclear, natural gas, diesel). However, even solar (plus storage) generated in large power plants will not be able to compete with on-site (rooftop) solar (plus storage). This is an architectural disruption. The reason is that on-site generation and storage does not need the expensive transmission infrastructure needed to bring energy generated at large-scale centralized plants to where the demand is.

Other models

Systemic disruption: Disruptions can potentially have devastating effects far beyond a single market category, causing whole sectors of the economy to be disrupted as a result. TaaS using on-demand, electric autonomous vehicles is not just disruptive to the ICE car manufacturing industry. It also has devastating effects on the oil industry as well as parking, insurance, car leasing and car dealerships.

Like dominoes falling, it may also trigger dramatic impacts on shipping, logistics, real estate, and infrastructure, and the bond and equity markets. Tens of trillions of dollars (beyond vehicles) may be at stake because of the TaaS disruption.

Business model innovation: Business model innovation is every bit as disruptive as technology innovation. A business model includes the core logic and strategic choices for creating and capturing value within a value network.[198] A business model innovation is a novel way of creating value and capturing value within a value network that is made possible by a technology convergence.

Disruptive business models may have a totally new logic and new set of metrics that change the basis of competition, and make it extremely difficult (or even impossible) for incumbents to adapt or to win.

For example, ride-hailing (Uber, Lyft, Didi) is a business model innovation enabled by the convergence of smartphones and the Cloud. This convergence enabled instant connections and geographic matching between individual passengers and drivers with spare capacity in a highly efficient, convenient and cost-effective way. Ride-hailing (also called ride-sharing) companies applied a brokerage business model by taking a cut of every transaction.

Similarly, Airbnb is a business model disruption. Another example: the solar energy industry in U.S. residential and commercial markets grew exponentially after the introduction of a new business model called zero-money-down solar. In this model, the solar provider would finance, install and even own the solar panels. Traditionally, homeowners had to purchase the panels upfront. But the new business model allowed them to purchase or lease them like they did a car: with no or little money down, and agreeing to a set monthly payment for several years.

Note that the business models don't have to be entirely new. Uber and Airbnb use the age-old brokerage business model, while solar borrowed the car lease and car loan models that have been used in the auto industry for a century. These business models were used in new settings to solve different problems, and were made possible by technology convergences.

Value network: Disruptors may leverage portions of existing value networks — a connected series of organizations, resources and knowledge streams involved in the creation and delivery of value to end customers — within and outside the industry they are disrupting, and/or create totally new networks that bypass the incumbents and reach customers in new ways. For instance, Tesla used the value network of the consumer electronics industry to source its batteries, hired people from the computer and auto industries, and created its own stores to reach customers directly, bypassing the auto industry's dealer channel.

Metrics: Disruptive business models may create a totally new set of metrics that change the basis of competition and make it extremely difficult (or even impossible) for incumbents to adapt or to win. New industries create new metrics for success. Companies measure themselves and organize their resources around those metrics, and the market rewards companies that are best at optimizing those metrics. As an example, the music industry traditionally measured success as a function of album or CD units sold. These metrics dominated over other indicators (e.g., number of songs per album or number of times songs were played). Industry awards were created to reward those who maximized those metrics: Gold Records (500,000 sold) or Platinum Records (1 million sold) were designed to reward recording artists who maximized those metrics. The advent of Internet streaming (or music as a service) disrupted this metric, ushering in a new key metric: number of plays per song. This new metric changed the basis of competition, bringing with it a totally new set of industry dynamics. Music-industry CD revenues plunged 84% in one decade, from $9.4 billion in 2006 to $1.5 billion in 2015, driven by on-demand streaming music.[199] Streaming came "out of nowhere" to generate $2.4 billion. Streaming companies are software companies with zero marginal costs that generate revenues with a number of business models. By one measurement, it takes 1,500 streams to equal the revenues of one album sale.[200] Traditional companies pushing CDs cannot possibly compete with streaming. Companies that organize themselves around pushing CDs cannot possibly compete in the new business environment. Similarly, Software as a Service (SaaS) companies (like Salesforce.com) ushered in new metrics that traditional software companies (like Oracle and SAP) could not compete with. They had to adapt or die.

Product innovation: Technology convergence makes it possible for companies to design products and services that solve customer problems in new ways. These products may have capabilities that create value in completely and heretofore unimaginable new ways, and they may make it impossible for incumbent products to compete.

The NEST Learning thermostat is an example. The convergence of sensors, mobile communications, computing, artificial intelligence, and the cloud made the product possible. The NEST learns users' patterns and behaviors and adjusts temperatures automatically to match their comfort levels. To minimize energy usage, the thermostat adjusts the temperature when the user leaves for work. An app that runs on smartphones makes it possible for the user to tell the thermostat to turn the heater or air conditioner on or off remotely. Using sensors, the NEST knows when a user is home, and uses artificial intelligence to adjust temperatures accordingly. It also has the capability to communicate with the utility to learn electricity prices, and to switch the heater and air conditioner on and off to save money while keeping temperatures within user comfort ranges. For instance, in the summer, it can "pre-cool" a home before the daily peak pricing period starts, and then turn the air conditioner on and off to maintain a comfortable temperature range while saving the owner money. Traditional thermostats could not possibly do this. Additionally, the thermostat communicates with the NEST Protect smoke and carbon monoxide detector. For example, upon learning from Protect that there is a carbon monoxide leak, the thermostat can shut down the furnace, a potential cause of the leak.[201]

Conceptual innovation: New concepts, methods, models, frameworks and software architectures enable totally new ways of doing things. Packet switching led to the development of the Internet Protocol Suite (commonly known as TCP/IP or Transmission Control Protocol / Internet Protocol), a new conceptual model of communications that led to the development of the internet.[202] Blockchain is an open, shared, immutable, distributed ledger for recording the history of transactions (blocks).[203] Like the internet, Blockchain is a conceptual innovation that can enable a wide range of new uses that were not possible before. For instance, when Blockchain converges with technologies such as distributed solar PV, batteries, sensors, mobile communications and artificial intelligence, it could enable new forms of transactions between devices within the home and between neighbors, and cities — where the metric of value is a kilowatt-hour, rather than a dollar or a Euro – while bypassing the utility (or the government) as the centralized trusted payment intermediary. Conceptually, this could never have been done before, but now trust can be distributed and transaction sizes can be dramatically smaller and cheaper when using Blockchain.

Open access technology development (OATD): Open access allows knowledge, skills, data, technologies, inventions and products to be developed at an increasingly faster and potentially disruptive pace. Open access to capital enables entrepreneurs to create products that would otherwise not have been funded by traditional investors.

The following are dimensions of an open access technology development ecosystem that can contribute to the acceleration of disruptions:

- Open **data** (Example: Climate.com)

- Open **content** (Wikipedia, Safecast)

- Open **knowledge** (Udacity, Coursera, Kahn)

- Open-source **software** (Android, Linux)

- Open-source **development/collaboration** (GitHub)

- Open-crowd **product development** (Quirky)

- Open **innovation** (Innocentive)

- Open **research** (Materials Project)

- Open **business models** (MySQL, RedHat)

- Open **APIs** (Google Maps, OpenAI)

- Open **funding**/crowd funding (Kickstarter, Indiegogo)

Open access lowers barriers to entry and lowers the cost and increases the speed of product development. It also reduces the ability of established companies to defend market positions, pricing power, and longevity of cash flows from existing products and services. Open access reduces advantages of scale, and reduces the need for corporations to build technology in-house. It allows anyone, anywhere to compete, leading to a dramatic increase in the number of competitors – and potential disruptors.

Silicon Valley is an example of an **open access technology development ecosystem** (OATDE) that combines the above dimensions within one geography. But the benefits and disruptive power of OATDE are spread around the world. For instance, the exponential growth in robotics development over the last decade has been enabled by an open-source operating system called ROS or Robot Operating System. ROS was initially developed at Stanford

University and is now managed by the Open Source Robotics Foundation.[204] Anybody anywhere around the world can download ROS for free and use it to create a new robot. Companies from MIT spinoff startup RethinkRobotics to French humanoid robot developer Aldebaran have used ROS to develop robots for different uses and industries. If an engineer needs to learn artificial intelligence for robotics, she can go online to a website such as Udacity and take a free course offered by Georgia Tech.[205] And while she's at it, she can learn how to program a self-driving car, and maybe win $100,000 in the process.[206] There are almost no barriers to a smart, committed engineer learning artificial intelligence and robotics to develop an autonomous vehicle. After doing that, it is possible to raise funds on a site like Kickstarter to take the product to the next level. If the entrepreneur wants to develop the whole vehicle, she can go to OSVehicle.com and use its open-source electric vehicle hardware platform.[207] One hour of assembly required. A small team of engineers based purely on OATDE can disrupt a billion-dollar car company in Detroit, Toyoda, or Wolfsburg. This team can learn artificial intelligence for free, use free operating systems that they learned to program for free, access open-source electric vehicle hardware platforms, and raise money openly on a crowdfunding site.

Market and systems dynamics: Markets are complex adaptive systems. In complex systems, causal relationships are seldom (if ever) linear, and changes in single variables can trigger quick, exponential and massive effects. Technology markets are made even more complex as many technologies changing at different rates converge, enabling products and business models that were once impossible to develop or even conceive. Open technology development accelerates these converging interrelationships even further. Additionally, technology markets have characteristics such as increasing returns, network effects, and adoption characteristics that enable disruptions to happen at increasingly faster rates and in ways that industrial-era resource-based industries cannot comprehend, let alone compete with. That's because mainstream analysts tend to see markets as stable, linear, and relatively simple systems.

A reason for linear thinking is that the industrial era relied on supply-side economies of scale. Known simply as "economies of scale," this norm posited that companies (and industries) gain cost advantage based on increased output, size, or scale of production.[208] The larger you are, the more you produce, the less the unit of output costs. This in turn gives the company an advantage in the marketplace. Industrial-era businesses such as car companies, steel manufacturers, and conventional power-plant operators run by this principle: bigger is better.

Technology markets flip that equation because of information economics. Demand-side economies of scale are a function of the number of users, rather than the number of units of production. The more users a product or company has, the more utility it generates, both for other users and for the company that offers the product. Google search is an example: the more users use its search engine, the more data it generates, the more it learns, the more knowledge it generates, and the better its products get for all users, which leads more users to use it, and so on. That is, Google's search engine exhibits increasing returns: each additional unit of output is cheaper to produce than the previous one. Google's value does not derive from the company's massive data centers, but from the users of its search engine.

In his 2006 book "Winners Take All," Seba described many characteristics of technology markets that created winners such as Apple, Google, Netflix, and Salesforce.com that have created platforms that exhibit increasing returns. There are no limits to the growth of knowledge, which makes these companies extremely valuable, especially when compared with traditional industrial and extractive industries. These four companies alone have created more than $1 trillion in wealth since Seba published "Winners Take All." Not coincidentally, several of these companies are also developing some of the key technologies that are enabling the disruption of transportation described in this report.

Network effects: Demand-side economies of scale become powerful when users are inter-connected in networks. The value of the underlying network can grow exponentially with the number of users and connections that they have with one another. Think of the original telephone, or email network, or Facebook. If one person has a telephone or email or Facebook, it's useless. When a second person joins the network, then you can connect with one person. Once a third user adopts, then each existing user can connect with two people. By the time a tenth user joins the network, each user can connect with nine other people, and the total combination of possible calls, emails, or connections is about 90. Once the millionth person joins, there are just under one trillion possible connections. Note two things: the first is that each time a new user adopts the technology, the value of the network increases for existing users. They get more value at no cost to them. Secondly, the value of the network increases exponentially; i.e., the formula is calculated to be around N^2 - N, where N is the number of users (this is called Metcalfe's Law).

Network effects virtually guarantee winner-take-all markets. There's no number-two network to Facebook. Operating systems like Microsoft Windows, Apple iOS, and Google Android have network effects. The value of the operating system increases with the number of users, which attracts software developers who create apps, which attract even more users, and so on, driving exponential growth in value. This virtuous cycle of value creation is the reason Apple, Google, Facebook and Microsoft have market valuations of hundreds of billions of dollars. In fact, these four companies plus Amazon are the five most valuable companies in the world, with a combined $2.6 trillion in market valuation (as of March 27, 2017).[209]

Technology adoption lifecycle S-curve: When Steve Jobs launched the Apple iPhone in 2007, mainstream experts and analysts from Bloomberg BusinessWeek to the Capital Group didn't give it a chance. Bloomberg's analyst wrote: "The iPhone's impact will be minimal. It will only appeal to a few gadget freaks. Nokia and Motorola haven't a care in the world."[210] Ten years later, there are 2.6 billion smartphones globally.[211] Whole industries have been launched because of the smartphone, and we could not imagine life without it.

Mainstream experts fail to appreciate that the technology adoption lifecycle is exponential, not linear. Adoption proceeds along an S-curve, where the early adopters who represent a small percent of the market set the stage for massive exponential growth as soon as the early mainstream users adopt a product or service.

Now that the smartphone has become a mainstream product, the expectation is that 6.1 billion users will have one by 2020.[212] The total world population is expected to be 7.6 billion by 2020.[213] That is, nearly every woman, man, and child on earth will use a smartphone just 13 years after its introduction. Not bad for a product whose impact was expected to be "minimal" by mainstream analysts.

RethinkTransportation

» About the Authors

Tony Seba

Tony Seba is a world-renowned thought leader, Silicon Valley entrepreneur, educator and the author of the Amazon #1 best-selling book *Clean Disruption of Energy and Transportation: How Silicon Valley Will Make Oil, Nuclear, Natural Gas, Coal, Electric Utilities and Conventional Cars Obsolete by 2030.* Tony's work focuses on the convergence of technologies, business models, and product innovations that disrupt the world's major industries. He was an early employee of disruptive companies including Cisco Systems and RSA Data Security. As a speaker he has delivered keynotes for major companies and at global events including Google, J.P. Morgan, CLSA Investors Forum, Intersolar, Davos, COP21 World Climate Summit and the Global Leaders Forum. Tony has taught thousands of entrepreneurs and corporate leaders at Stanford University Continuing Studies. He earned a Stanford MBA and a Computer Science and Engineering degree from the Massachusetts Institute of Technology.

James Arbib

James Arbib is a London-based investor in technology. He is the founder of Tellus Mater, an independent philanthropic foundation dedicated to exploring the impacts of disruptive technology, and its potential for solving some of the world's most challenging problems. In addition, Arbib oversees a London-based family office with a diversified portfolio, across all asset classes and a focus on the risks and opportunities of technology disruption. A graduate in History from Trinity College, Cambridge, Arbib has a Masters in Sustainability Leadership also from Cambridge. He is a qualified chartered accountant and worked as an investment analyst covering Utilities.

» List of Figures

» Endnotes

S-curve acceleration: The adoption S-curve has accelerated over time. It took the telephone 75 years to reach 50 million users. Radio reached 50 million in about half the time: 38 years. The television did it in a third of the time it took the radio -- 13 years -- while the computer tablet reached 50 million in about a sixth of the time it took the radio: two years.[214] The rate of acceleration has itself accelerated.

1   Challer, Bruce. 2017. Turns out, Uber is clogging the streets. *New York Daily News,* February 27.

2   Please see S-Curve graph in Seba Technology Disruption Framework, pag 12.

3   U.S. Bureau of Economic Analysis. Personal Consumption Expenditures and Gross Domestic Product. Retrieved from FRED, Federal Reserve Bank of St. Louis.

4   There are many potential new business opportunities that might be unleashed by low cost transport. We use "Starbucks on wheels" as an example. If cost per passenger mile drops to 2-3c by 2030, the economics of running a Starbucks on wheels on popular routes might become hugely favorable compared to the cost of the real estate investment needed in city-center stores. If a 20-seater vehicle costing 2 cents per passenger mile covered 100,000 miles per year, the cost of the vehicle would be $40,000 per year, substantially less than the equivalent rent on a store. A Starbucks van could operate on popular routes, subsidizing travel costs through the sale of food and beverage. As autonomous technology begins processing costumer data sources, such as social media, marketing and e-commerce could also become potential venues for revenue generation.

5   Challer. 2017.

6   This is in line with announcements made by Ford, BMW, Toyota, Audi, and Nissan to launch self-driving cars by 2021 (Muoio, D. 2017. These 19 Companies Are Racing to Build Self-Driving Cars in The Next 5 Years. *Business Insider UK,* January 12. Other industry sources forecast an earlier date than 2021. For instance, Elon Musk announced that Tesla would produce a self-driving car that could travel between Los Angeles and New York by the end of 2017 (Stewart, J. 2016. Tesla's Self-Driving Car Plan Seems Insane, But It Just Might Work. *Wired,* October 24. In partnership with Lyft, GM will begin providing ride sharing services with thousands of self-driving Chevy Bolt electric vehicles in early 2018 (Fortune. 2017. GM and Lyft Plan to Deploy Thousands of Self-Driving Chevy Bolts. February 17. Rocky Mountain Institute estimates on-demand mobility services provided by autonomous vehicles will be available by 2018 (Johnson, C. and

Walker, J. 2016. *Peak Car Ownership: Market Opportunity of Electric Automated Mobility Services*. Rocky Mountain Institute. Retrieved from here).

7   This is based on our calculations for average household expenditures on travel. American households own an average of 1.9 cars, and each car travels an average of 11,300 miles a year. In our model, the cost of travel by TaaS is 15.9 cents per vehicle mile, therefore average household expenditure comes down to $3,400. Source: US Bureau of Transport Statistics. 2001. *National Household Travel Survey*.

8   U.S. Bureau of Labor Statistics (BLS). 2015, U.S. average household spending on all except public transport in 2015. *Consumer Expenditure Survey 2015*. August.

9   The spike in IO ICE and EV costs between 2021-4 are related to the depreciation cost treatment. As TaaS becomes available and users begin to switch, there will be a surplus of used cars on the market, and a fall in demand for them. We see residual values for these vehicles dropping which affects the cost-per-mile,

10   These figures for cost in 2030 do not consider the diseconomies of scale or other negative feedback loops that might occur as new ICE sales decline and costs of ownership rise.

11   TaaS Pool figures are for cost per passenger mile; other costs are all cost per vehicle mile.

12   In this comparison, we adjust the A-ICE Platform cost to be the same as the A-EV cost as opposed to applying the same 20% of cost-per-mile charge, which would lead to a proportionately higher charge for the A-ICE platform.

13   Based on an interview with Rahul Sonnad, CEO Tesloop.

14   The battery of this Tesloop vehicle was replaced at 200,000 miles, but this was due to a software fault that affected the fuel gauge.

15   Tesloop charges its vehicles up to 5 times per day to 100% using superchargers. Although fast charging degrades the battery faster, the company made a strategic decision to move the vehicles with degraded batteries to shorter trips. To date, Tesloop has not needed to put this strategy into practice.

16   At this level, Tesloop expects battery degradation of 30%. Our model assumes end of battery life at 20% degradation.

17   Tesloop also had some problems with lights due to high-water floods.

18   There are many potential new business opportunities that might be unleashed by low cost transport. We use "Starbucks on wheels" as an example. If cost per passenger mile drops to 2-3c by 2030, the economics of running a 'Starbucks on wheels' on popular routes might become hugely favorable compared to the cost of the real estate investment needed in city-center stores. If a 20-seater vehicle costing 2 cents per passenger mile covered 100,000 miles per year, the cost of the vehicle would be $40,000 per year, substantially less than the equivalent rent on a store. A Starbucks van could operate on popular routes, subsidizing travel costs through the sale of food and beverage. As autonomous technology begins processing costumer data sources, such as social media, marketing and e-commerce could also become potential venues for revenue generation.

19   The U.S. electricity demand data points refers to peak demand on February 3 and August 3 in 2016. US EIA. 2016. *US*

Electricity Demand and Supply Balance. Retrieved on February 22, 2017.

20   The calculation of 200GWh is simply 4 million batteries x 60kWh each x 80% (rounded). U.S. draws 640GW maximum and an average of 500GW. For eight-hour storage, you would need $8 \times 500 = 4{,}000$GWh.

21   U.S. Department of Energy. 2013. *Grid Storage*. December.

22   Seba, Tony. 2006. *Winners Take All — The 9 Fundamental Rules of High Tech Strategy*. Amazon Digital Services LLC.

23   Pension Rights Center. Income of Today's Older Adults.

24   Malito, Alessandra. 2017. Why American millennials may never get to live alone. Market Watch, March 19.

25   Boak, Josh. 2015. 1-in-4 US renters spend half their pay on rent and utilities. Associated Press, May 1.

26   Trialability is ease of testing or using a product or service. See Rogers, E. M. 2003. *Diffusion of Innovations*. New York: Free Press.

27   Peteraf, M. 1993. The Cornerstones of Competitive Advantage: A Resource-Based View. *Strategic Management Journal* 14(3): 179-191.

28   Laing, Keith. 2016. Obama pledges nearly $4 billion for self-driving cars. *The Hill*, January 14.

29   National Highway Traffic Safety Administration. Automated Vehicles.

30   California Department of Motor Vehicles. Testing of Autonomous Vehicles. Accessed April 19, 2017.

31   Burgess, Matt. 2017. California could get truly driverless cars with new rules.

Wired, March 13.

32   This assumes the comparison is with TaaS Private and not TaaS Pool. The figure of $1 trillion for 2030 is based on an even split of miles between TaaS Private and TaaS Pool.

33   U.S. Bureau of Economic Analysis, Personal Consumption Expenditures and Gross Domestic Product. Retrieved from FRED, Federal Reserve Bank of St. Louis.

34   Bloomberg New Energy Finance. 2016. Electric vehicles to be 35% of global new car sales by 2040. February 25.

35   The average price of a new car or truck sold in the U.S. in 2015 was $33,560. (Kelley Blue Book. 2016).

36   Lead times on opening battery factories is short, with most estimates we have received from experts being under 1 year for the opening of Giga-scale factories. The major constraint on battery factories is material supply. Tony Seba and Simon Moores, Benchmark Minerals.

37   U.S. Geological Survey 2017. *Lithium*.

38   Lithium is a relatively abundant resource, found in many parts of the world. The countries with the largest reserves are currently focused in Bolivia and Chile. But it is found also in Canada, Russia, China, and parts of Africa (U.S. Geological Survey, 2017). Under our TaaS scenario, global TaaS vehicle production would be 28 million by 2030. By 2030, batteries will require 0.6kg of Lithium per kWh — an improvement from 0.8kg currently (Interview with Simon Moores, Benchmark Minerals, January 2017). The average battery size is 60 kWh in our model, meaning each car would need 36kg of Lithium. Annual lithium requirements would be 1 million tons per year (assuming no

recycling). Current global identified resources are over 40m tons, though we expect market forces to drive more to be discovered and added to reserves as production increases. Even with an increase in rebound effect as transport becomes rapidly more affordable in developing countries, given the timescales involved, we would expect lithium supply to be able to match demand. Lithium demand in our model is within the constraint identified by our experts.

39   *The Economist*. 2016. Uberworld. September 3.

40   As an example, a large percentage of the revenues and profits in newspaper publishing shrunk dramatically in the decade after Google created AdWords (in 2000), while trillions in new wealth was created by online news-providing companies including Alphabet (Google), Facebook and Baidu.

41   As an example, the music industry traditionally measured success as a function of album or CD units sold. These metrics dominated over other indicators (e.g., number of songs per album/CD, number of times songs were played). The advent of internet streaming (or music as a service) disrupted the metric (to number of plays per song) as well as music industry dynamics, business innovation and revenue models.

42   These changes in metrics also act as pointers to the underlying dynamics of the disruption, which will be characterized by a new focus on asset (vehicle) efficiency, business model innovation (the rise of platform-based TaaS providers) and new revenue streams (the new customer-facing per-mile charges).

43   The 97 million IO vehicles represent the surplus of passenger miles in the IO vehicle stock divided by 11,300 (the average current vehicle miles per year). It is possible that not all these vehicles will be stranded, and the "surplus" miles that the IO stock has available is met by more vehicles doing less than 11,300 miles, and thus more vehicles are partially stranded.

44   As new car sales for any given year are defined as the difference between vehicle stock capacity and the demand for passenger miles, no new ICE vehicles will therefore be sold into mainstream markets from 2024 onwards. Just as there are niche players who manufacture vinyl records and turntables in the Internet streaming era, so there may still be ICE cars manufactured by small niche players. This might derive from demand from collectors, from consumers who are not price sensitive, and from those who live in areas where TaaS adoption is slow (e.g., remote rural regions). However, this demand is likely to be negligible. The overall implication is that the capacity of the ICE value chain to survive, given the scale of disruption, will be terminally impaired.

45   This would create a vicious cycle that accelerates the demise of the ICE car manufacturing industry. For example, once the resale value of a new ICE car is assumed to be zero or even negative, the monthly payments for a new ICE car would rise dramatically. Negative used ICE car prices would make more economic sense to potential buyers than purchasing a new ICE car, even if running costs are higher. The implication of our modeling is that new ICE cars would make no economic sense under any circumstance – plunging the industry into a death spiral.

46 This at first sight seems counter-intuitive, given that ICEs in 2030 still represent 40% of all vehicles in use; but the decline in their numbers is a function of vehicle lifecycle. Additionally, the end of ICEs may happen more quickly, as a function of the implosion of the overall ICE vehicle stock, or because of a TaaS enabling policy environment (see Part 1) in which moves to ban ICEs gain traction.

47 Bomey, Nathan. Average age of cars on U.S. roads breaks record. USA Today. July 29, 2015.

48 TaaS providers (or the fleet owners from whom they lease) will purchase A-EVs direct from manufacturers, with financing and maintenance carried out by themselves (or outsourced to large and specialized companies). The result will be that the traditional roles of car dealers will be taken over by TaaS providers/fleet owners. We therefore see the car dealership industry in terminal decline from the advent of the TaaS disruption, with virtual cessation likely within no more than 3-4 years from that date, apart from the small residual niche requirement for the rapidly shrinking fleet of ICE vehicles.

49 These drivers of lower insurance are also likely to act as catalysts for a shift from opacity to transparency in premium pricing. For example, a portion of premiums is currently charged as a function of assumptions that penalize certain groups (e.g., negative assumptions relating to zip codes, driver age and ethnicity), regardless of consumer driving records. Such considerations will be likely to diminish or even evaporate within the TaaS model, because of per-mile rather than per-owner charges, although some loading for TaaS travel in deprived neighborhoods may continue. Other factors exerting downward pressure on insurance industry margins will be the dramatically higher buying power that TaaS providers/fleet owners will have, relative to individual buyers, and the ways in which real-time data (e.g., from sensors in A-EVs) can be used to analyze driving patterns and risks, thus increasing transparency within premium pricing. The likely outcome is that incumbent insurance companies which resist TaaS (by seeking to maintain margins and obsolete pricing models) will face severe threats to their survival, because TaaS providers will have the option of self-insuring. In overall terms, the passenger miles' metric will emerge as the key pricing tool for a new breed of insurance companies.

50 Our modeling indicates that a 1 cent per mile tax would raise about the same revenue as gasoline taxes raises today: $45 billion in 2015 growing to $63 billion in 2030 taxes (author's calculation). Whether to tax an emerging industry is for policymakers and citizens to decide. Internet commerce, for instance, remained largely untaxed until it became a substantial industry. A one-cent-a-mile tax might sound very modest, but our findings indicate that the cost of a TaaS passenger mile will fall to about 5 cents per mile in 2030, implying a 20% tax on passenger road transportation. Given the societal gains from TaaS (e.g., health improvements from cleaner air, fewer accidents, emissions reductions), a per-mile TaaS tax might be viewed as regressive and counter-productive for society's well-being.

51 The winners of the operating system wars over the last few decades have created franchises worth hundreds of billions of dollars. Microsoft was the world's most valuable company

due to owning DOS and Windows, the operating systems that ran personal computers for three decades. Apple is the world's most valuable company today because it owns iOS, the operating system that runs its iPhones and iPads. Google/Alphabet, one of the world's most valuable companies, owns Android, which runs most smartphones and tablets without an Apple logo. Cisco owns the most successful operating system of the Internet. It was briefly the world's most valuable company, and it is still worth hundreds of billions of dollars (Seba, T. 2006. *Winners Take All: The 9 Fundamental Rules for High Tech Strategy*. Amazon Digital Services LLC.).

52   Hull, D. 2016. The Tesla Advantage: 1.3 Billion Miles of Data. *Bloomberg*, December 20.

53   Stewart, J. 2016. Tesla's Self-Driving Car Plan Seems Insane, But It Just Might Work. *Wired*, October 24.

54   Muoio, D. 2016. Tesla Just Made a Big Move to Take On Uber. *Business Insider UK*, October 26.

55   Newcomer, E. 2016. GM Invests $500 Million in Lyft. *Bloomberg*, January 04.

56   Hanley, S. 2016. BMW to Launch 40 Self-Driving Cars in Preparation for Ride Sharing Service. *Teslarati*, December 06.

57   Nicola, S. 2016. Daimler Boosts Blacklane Stake as Ride-Sharing Market Heats Up. *Bloomberg*, August 01.

58   Uber's one million drivers were logging one hundred million miles per day. (Chafkin, M. 2016. Uber's First Self-Driving Fleet Arrives in Pittsburgh This Month. *Bloomberg*, August 18). Tesla vehicles have logged nearly 4 billion miles, a number that grows each second. The company provides a real-time counter that shows the number of miles driven by its vehicles (Tesla. 2016. The Electric Road Trip).

59   Hawkins, A. 2017. Tesla's Crash Rate Dropped 40 Percent After Autopilot Was Installed, Feds Say. *The Verge*, January 19.

60   King, I. and Copolla, G. 2017. Intel to Buy Mobileye for About $15 Billion Car Tech Push. *Bloomberg*, March 13.

61   U.S. Bureau of Transportation Statistics. 2017. *National Transportation Statistics*. Table 1-40: U.S. Passenger-Miles (Millions). See also, Bureau of Transportation Statistics, National Household Travel Survey Daily Travel Quick Facts, 2002.

62   Lee, D. 2016. Tony Seba Predicts the Internal Combustion Engine Will Be Obsolete by 2030 – Why? What Are the Implications? *Value Innovations*, January 17.

63   Brian, M. 2017. Samsung EV Battery Offers 500 km Range with 20 Minutes of Charge. *Engadget*, January 09.

64   Ayre, J. 2015. 10 Biggest Electric Car Battery Manufacturers Are... *Clean Technica*, May 6.

65   Carson, B. 2016. 2016. Uber Has Quietly Launched its Own 'Uber for Trucking' Marketplace Called Uber Freight. *Business Insider UK*, October 26.

66   Torrey, F., and Murray, D. 2015. *An Analysis of the Operational Costs of Trucking: 2015 Update*. American Transportation Research Institute, September. Arlington, Virginia.

67   Punte, S. 2009. *Opportunities and Challenges for Fuel and Emissions Reductions in Trucks in China and Asia*.

Clean Air Initiative for Asian Cities Center.

68   Evangelist, J. 2016. Improving Fleet Utilization: Getting to 100%. *Fleet Owner*, December 12.

69   Grobart, S. 2015. Daimler Veers into Maximum Overdrive: The Company's Self-Driving Freightliner Truck Hits the Road. *Bloomberg*, May 14.

70   Dillet, R. 2016. Uber Acquires Otto to Lead Uber's Self-Driving Car Effort. *Tech Crunch*, August 16.

71   U.S. Department of Transportation. 2015. *Freight Facts and Figures 2015*.

72   This range is well within what Tesla vehicles offer today. By the time the disruption of A-EVs kicks in, the cost of batteries for trucks with a range of more than 1,000 miles will be a fraction of their cost today. The 71% figure also represents a critical mass of adopters who would attract market players to make capital investments in a national fast charging network for trucks, possibly collocated at today's truck stops.

73   BYD. 2017. K11 Electric Transit Bus.

74   Davis, S.C. and Williams, S.E. 2016. Table 1.16 Transportation Petroleum Use by Mode, 2013-2014. In *Transportation Energy Data Book*. Oak Ridge National Laboratory.

75   This is a provisional forecast, and is less developed than our core passenger vehicle analysis. We will have a more granular forecast in future versions of this study.

76   U.S. Energy Information Administration. 2015. Oil: Crude and Petroleum Products Explained.

77   Econtrader. 2014. How much gasoline does a barrel of crude oil produce.

78   Canadian Fuels Association. *The Economics of Petroleum Refining - Understanding the business of processing crude oil into fuels and other value added products*. December 2013.

79   Nelson, B. 2013. Black secures $25 billion for Kitimat oil refinery. Business Vancouver, March 11.

80   Refinery Retrofit. 2006. Montreal Gazette, September 21.

81   Cash cost is defined as investments (well and facility) and operational (taxes, SG&A, transportation, production) costs.

82   Ghaddar, A. 2017. Oil Overhang Points to Need for Extended OPEC Output Cuts. *Reuters*, February 10.

83   Randall, T. 2016. Here's How Electric Cars Will Cause the Next Oil Crisis. *Bloomberg*, February 25.

84   Clark, P., Campbell, P. 2016. Motor Industry: Pressure On the Pump. *Financial Times*, August 30.

85   Kemp, J. 2015. The Oil Crash Explained: John Kemp On The 5 Causes That Led to Oil's Decline. *Reuters*, February 9.

86   The latter would have consequences not only in oil markets but also in bond markets. That is, these countries would either borrow to invest in their oil sector or stop servicing their debts to redirect treasury cash to subsidize their oil industry to keep it afloat. This would exacerbate the vicious cycle of the disruption: the market gets flooded with uneconomically produced oil, which depresses prices further, leading governments to borrow more (and/ or stop servicing more of their debt) to plug the ever-widening cash holes in

their treasuries.

87   Saudi Arabia, Iran, Iraq, Kuwait, Qatar and the U.A.E. will be affected oil producers in the Gulf region.

88   Data for Venezuela and Angola for 2014 was not available in the World Bank database.

89   Our analysis indicates that the total potential commercial oil from the top 20 Bakken producers would be 480,000 bpd. There is already 763,000 bpd of pipeline capacity plus 108,000 bpd of refining capacity serving Bakken oil. Under our model, there would be pipeline overcapacity in Bakken even without DAPL. Projects like DAPL were financed under mainstream business-as-usual oil volume growth assumptions. But under our model, DAPL would have to carry all of Bakken's potential oil production to fill its pipes. This is not likely to happen in a market with that much excess pipeline capacity.

90   Levin, S. 2016. Dakota Access Pipeline: The Who, What and Why of the Standing Rock Protests. *The Guardian*, November 03.

91   As more projects are stranded in the Canadian tar sands, the need for pipelines to transport the vanishing oil also evaporates. Projects such as the Keystone XL Pipeline, whose financial viability depends on the assumption of high volumes being transported from Canada to Louisiana and Texas, would therefore become a financially dubious undertaking and possibly a stranded asset. Similarly, the refineries in Louisiana and Texas that focus on refining oil sands would see volumes trickle down and become financially unviable.

92   U.S. Department of State (DOS). 2014. *Final Supplemental Environmental Impact Statement for the Keystone XL Project.* January.

93   A barrel of oil has a number of constituent parts. The disruption to the gasoline and diesel element might lead to a shortage of other constituent parts of the barrel, requiring retrofitting of refineries or reprocessing of gasoline and diesel, or even the refining of surplus crude to meet the demands for non-gasoline fractions.

94   Companies in the oil field services are likely to face a disproportionately large exposure to high-cost projects that will be stranded by the demand disruption.

95   Phillips, E. and Jackson, P. 2015. *Beyond Cost Cutting: The Opportunity for Oilfield Services and Equipment Companies.* Bain & Company, December 02.

96   Shell. 2016. Capital Markets Day 2016: Re-shaping Shell to Create a World Class Investment Case. July 07.

97   Katakey, R., Hoffman, A. and Rascouet, A. 2017. Shell Sells $4.7 Billions of Fields as Disposals Accelerate. *Bloomberg*, January 31.

98   Katakey, R., Jordan, A. 2017. Shell Cuts Debt with $7.25 Billion Sale of Canada Oil Sands. *Bloomberg*, March 9.

99   Martin, M. and Narayanan, A. 2017. Saudi Aramco Hires Banks for First Time Bond Sale Ahead of IPO. *Bloomberg*, February 06.

100 This is similar to the approach taken by certain utility companies such as E-On and RWE. Chazan, G. 2016. Eon and RWE Pursue Radical Restructurings. *Financial Times*, May 18.

101 Krauss, C. 2016. Exxon Concedes It May

Need to Declare Lower Value for Oil in Ground. *The New York Times*, October 28.

102 Several countries announced their plans for scaling up electric and self-driving vehicle sales. China put forward an ambitious plan to become a global leader of A-EVs, setting a target of 50% of new vehicle sales in partially autonomous vehicles by 2020 and 15% of sales in fully automated vehicles by 2025. While American companies are leading the technological innovation for now, China may head the curve with more autonomous vehicles on the road by 2020. European countries also support the dissemination of EVs. Norway set the goal of 100% of new car sales to be zero-emissions vehicles from 2025 on. The Norwegian government passed a VAT exemption for EV owners and other consumer incentives to achieve its target for EV sales by 2025. Athens, Madrid and Paris have announced bans on diesel vehicles on the road by 2025.

103 Fagnant, D. J. and Kockelman, K. M. 2014. The Travel and Environmental Implications of Shared Autonomous Vehicles, Using Agent-Based Model Scenarios. *Transportation Research Part C: Emerging Technologies* 40: 1-13.

104 Travelling a mile with TaaS Private by 2030 could cost the customer 10 cents (and as little as 3 cents with TaaS Pool), a significant reduction of the current cost of 62 cents under IO as of 2016. According to the U.S. Department of Transportation, the average American family spends 19% of its income on transportation (U.S. Department of Transportation. 2015. *Transportation and Housing Costs*.). Poor households spend a larger share of their income on transport.

105 Calculating the GDP gain: Americans today make a GDP per capita per working hour of $27. That is, the U.S. working population of 243 million worked 2,000 hours each to make $13 trillion during 2012. The TaaS disruption will free up a minimum of 87 billion hours of commuting time. If those hours generated the same $27 of GDP that they generate today, then this would create an incremental $2.3 trillion. However, it is unlikely that all these hours would be spent working. Discounting for relaxation time during TaaS journeys is necessary; in reality, many hours spent travelling under TaaS will not be economically productive, and thus a discount on the per-working-hour rate of basing the calculation on $28.60 is required. One approach would be to use the 8,760 hours of the year, per person, (which includes sleep, work, study, and leisure). The per-working-hour rate then falls to $6.63 in 2016. This would generate additional GDP of $575 billion.

106 Auto Alliance. 2016. America's Automobile Industry Is One of the Most Powerful Engines Driving the US Economy. January 26.

107 Greenhouse, S. 2016. Autonomous Vehicles Could Cost America 5 Million Jobs. What Should We Do About It? *LA Times*, September 22.

108 Futurism. 2017. Universal Basic Income: The Answer to Automation?.

109 Solon, O. 2016. Self-Driving Trucks: What's the Future for America's 3.5 Million Truckers? *The Guardian*, June 17.

110 For example, Tesla's Gigafactory in partnership with Panasonic will employ 6,500 people when at full capacity in 2018 (Tesla. 2014. Gigafactory. February 26). New jobs in services will also be created

from on-board digital media services, as well as in software development.

111 This figure is for heavy truck drivers. Bus drivers and van drivers earn less (U.S. Bureau of Labor Statistics (BLS). 2017. *Occupational Outlook Handbook.* Transportation and Material Moving Occupations).

112 Door-to-door and schedule-less travel services have been traditionally provided by human-driven taxis, which are relatively higher in cost compared to personal driving and public transport, and which have prevented large-scale uptake of on-demand services. TaaS will bring down the cost considerably, with no driver wage required and increased coordination across the fleet.

113 Travelling with Uber in New York currently has a waiting time of under 2 minutes, 25 seconds in Manhattan and 3 minutes, 8 seconds in outer boroughs (Mosendz, P. 2014. Here's How Long It Takes to Get An Uber in US Cities. *Newsweek*, April 12).

114 Access is defined as the number of inhabitants or points in a city reachable in a certain time (International Transport Forum (ITF). 2017. ITF Transport Outlook 2017).

115 U.S. Environmental Protection Agency (EPA). 2014. *Sources of Greenhouse Gas Emissions.*

116 Note that this includes both passenger cars and light-duty trucks.

117 U.S. Department of Transportation. 2006. *Transportation's Role in Climate Change.*

118 To reduce its economy-wide GHG emissions by 26-28% by 2025, compared to 2005 levels (US Department of State. 2015. *The United States' Intended Nationally Determined*

Contribution (INDC). March 31).

119 Achieving emissions reductions relies on the decarbonization of the electricity sector. A-EVs have zero tailpipe emissions when in operation, if the electricity powering their batteries is generated entirely from renewable energy. However, this is not the case if power is supplied from non-renewable sources. Achieving full decarbonization of passenger vehicles will rely on a concurrent switch to renewable electricity in fueling EVs.

120 Defined as the sum of electricity demand in the residential, commercial, industrial and transport sectors.

121 US EIA. 2017. Transportation: Travel Indicators: Light-Duty Vehicles = 8500 lbs. *In Annual Energy Outlook.*

122 When taking into account the weighted average of cars sold in each state in 2014, and the local electricity mix.

123 Anair, D., Nealer, R. and Reichmuth, D. 2015. *Cleaner Cars from Cradle to Grave, How Electric Cars Beat Gasoline Cars on Lifetime Global Warming Emission.* Union of Concerned Scientists..

124 ibid.

125 Helms, H., Pehnt, M., Lambrecht, U. and Liebich, A. 2010. Electric Vehicle and Plug-in Hybrid Energy Efficiency and Life Cycle Emissions. 18th International Symposium Transport and Air Pollution: 113–274.

126 Faias, S., Sousa, J., Xavier, L., Ferreira, P. 2011. Energy Consumption and CO2 Emissions Evaluation for Electric and Internal Combustion Vehicles using a LCA Approach. *International Conference on Renewable Energy and Power Quality* 1(9): 1382–1388.

127 Anair et al. (2015) mentions per-mile comparison, but use equal mileage due to data constraints.

128 Ayre, J. 2017. Tesla Gigafactory Rooftop Solar System To Be 7 Times Larger Than Largest Rooftop Solar System Today. *Clean Technica*. January 16.

129 Apple. 2016. Apple Joins RE100, Announces Supplier Clean Energy Pledges. September 19.

130 World Health Organization (WHO). 2016. *Ambient Air Pollution: A Global Assessment of Exposure and Burden of Disease.*

131 Measured by individuals' willingness to pay to reduce the risk of dying (OECD. 2014. *The Cost of Air Pollution: Health Impacts of Road Transport.* OECD Publishing, Paris).

132 World Health Organization. 2015. *Economic Cost of the Health Impact of Air Pollution in Europe: Clean Air, Health and Wealth.*

133 OECD. 2014. *The Cost of Air Pollution: Health Impacts of Road Transport.* OECD Publishing, Paris.

134 World Health Organization. 2015. *Global Status Report on Road Safety.*

135 Seba, T. 2014. *Clean Disruption of Energy and Transportation: How Silicon Valley Will Make Oil, Nuclear, Natural Gas, Coal, Electric Utilities and Conventional Cars Obsolete by 2030.* Clean Planet Ventures, California.

136 Noland, E. 2016. *Oil: Assessing Global Geopolitical Risks.* CME Group. August 31.

137 *Politico Magazine.* 2016. The Hidden Consequences of the Oil Crash. January 21.

138 U.S. Energy Information Administration (EIA).. 2016. *How Much Petroleum Does the United States Import and Export?* October 4.

139 Egbue, O. and Long, S. 2011. Critical Issues in the Supply Chain of Lithium for Electric Vehicle Batteries. *Engineering Management Journal* 24(3): 52-62.

140 Lithium reserves (million tons): Bolivia: 9, Chile: 7.5, US: 6.7, Argentina: 6.5, Australia: 1.7, and China: 5.1. U.S. Geological Survey. 2016. *Lithium.*

141 Reuters. 2016. What Price Lithium, the Metal of the Future? June 6.

142 Home, A. 2016. What Price Lithium, the Metal of the Future? *Reuters*, June 07.

143 Benchmark Minerals Intelligence. 2016. Elon Musk: Our Lithium-Ion Batteries Should Be Called Nickel – graphite. June 16.

144 Qnovo. 2016. The Cost Components of a Lithium-Ion Battery. January 11.

145 Lacey, S. 2016. "Stem CTO: Lithium-ion Battery Prices Fell 70% In The Last 18 Months." *Green Tech Media*, June 28.

146 Lithium and cobalt experts at Benchmark Minerals.

147 BYD. 2017. World's First Mass Produced 40Ft Long Range Battery-Electric Bus.

148 Will L. 2016. "Come as You Are – Lithium, Cobalt and Tesla's Battery Problem." *Harvard Business Review*, November 4.

149 Petersen, J. 2016. "Electric Vehicle Batteries Face Two Critical Mineral Constraints." *Seeking Alpha*, November 30.

150 Interview with Benchmark minerals experts, March 2017.

151 Burton, M. 2017. How Does the Hottest Metals Trade Work? First, Find Storage. *Bloomberg*, January 24.

152 Cobalt Blue Holdings. 2017. Cobalt.

153 This substitution involves a sacrifice in "specific power," which affects speed of acceleration. In a TaaS fleet, acceleration is a less-important vehicle attribute.

154 Power Technology. 2017. Buses and Batteries: A Rising Sector.

155 Lambert, F. 2016. Breakdown of Raw Materials in Tesla's Batteries and Possible Bottlenecks. *Electrek*, November 01.

156 Cardwell, D. 2016. GM and Nissan Reusing Old Electric Car Batteries. *The New York Times*, June 16.

157 McIntire-Strasburg, J. 2015. The Electric Vehicle Battery Can and Should Be Recycled. *Clean Technica*, July 23.

158 We include AV hardware and software as an addition to the upfront cost of the vehicles, using $5,000 as the cost in 2020, and apply a separate cost curve to this until 2030.

159 Battery lifetime is calculated in terms of cycles, and 80% capacity is the industry benchmark for battery capacity (Arcus, C. 2016. Battery Lifetime: How Long Can Electric Vehicle Batteries Last? *Clean Technica*, May 31).

160 UCLA Law and UC Berkeley School of Law. 2014. *Reuse and Repower: How to Save Money and Clean the Grid with Second-life Electric Vehicle Batteries*. September.

161 Ayre, J. 2016. Recycling EV Batteries More Cost-Competitive than Using for Home Energy Storage – Lux Research Echoes Tesla CTO JB Straubel. *Clean Technica*, November 24.

162 Data from high-utilization users of batteries suggest they are lasting far longer in the field than expected. Proterra sees a historical trend indicating a 5-6% improvement in cell performance each year. Chanje Energy (formerly Nohm) expects its batteries to last 500,000 miles by 2021. Tesloop expects them to last far longer. Interviews with Proterra, Chanje Energy and Tesloop, January-March 2017.

163 Lambert, F. 2016. Tesla Model S Battery Pack Data Shows Very Little Capacity Loss Over High Mileage. *Elecktrek*, June 16.

164 Confirmed in interviews with Chanje Energy and other sources such as *Industrial Minerals*. 2016. "Dissecting Lithium Battery Technology." June 02.

165 Depletion is when capacity drops below 80% of original capacity.

166 It should be noted that charge cycles are on the basis of full discharge and full charge cycles, which adversely affect battery lifetime-charging to 80% or less prolongs battery life beyond this. On the other side, charging by supercharger also reduces life cycles. Battery lifetime can also be affected by different environmental conditions and terrains.

167 *Industrial Minerals*. 2016. Dissecting lithium battery technology. June 02.

168 Interviews with Chanje Energy.

169 Interview with Tesloop CEO. Tesloop has a number of high-utilization Teslas that cover about 20k miles per month. Tesloop has seen very

limited degradation over 200,000 miles (approximately 6%), and expects batteries to last for at least 500,000 miles.

170 *Electric Vehicle News*. 2016. Chevy Bolt EV Requires Zero Maintenance. December 12.

171 Proterra. 2017. Unparalleled Durability.

172 Interviews with Proterra, Tesloop and Chanje.

173 According to a study using 2.5 million used-car sales on the automotive site iSeeCars.com, only 12.9% of sold cars are from the original owner after 10 years (Edgerton, J. 2017. Cars People Keep for 10 Years. CBS News, January 05. Retrieved from here).

174 In fact this is what Tesloop is doing. They operate a form of TaaS and depreciate the vehicles fully over 5 years (over 500,000 miles).

175 Chanje expect EVs to require 10% maintenance costs compared to ICE by 2021, Proterra expects maintenance costs to be <20% of conventional vehicles by 2021 and Tesloop 10% in 2017. Interviews with Proterra, Tesloop and Chanje.

176 Cartrack. 2016. Integrated Annual Report.

177 Viereckl, R., Ahleman, D., Koster, A., Jursch, S. 2015. *Connected Car Study 2015: Racing Ahead with Autonomous Cars and Digital Innovation*. Price Waters Coopers, December 16.

178 Interview with NVIDIA, January 2017.

179 Ramsey, M. 2015. Self-driving Cars Could Cut Down on Accidents, Study Says. *The Wall Street Journal*, March 5.

180 Securing America's Future Energy (SAE). *Commission on Autonomous Vehicle Testing and Safety*. 2017. January 5.

181 Hawkins, A. 2017. Tesla's Crash Rate Dropped 40 Percent After Autopilot Was Installed, Feds Say. *The Verge*, January 19.

182 Brian Wang. 2016. Intel will deliver 100X increase in deep learning training. *Next Big Future*, November 26.

183 *The Economist*. 2016. Autonomous Car Insurance: Look, No Claims! September 22.

184 Gonder, J., Earleywine, M., and Sparks, W. 2012. Analyzing Vehicle Fuel Saving Opportunities through Intelligent Driver Feedback. *SAE International Journal of Passenger Cars — Electronic Electrical Systems* 5(2):450-461.

185 20% refers to the average platform cost charged by Uber (Johnson, C. and Walker, J. 2016. *Peak Car Ownership: Market Opportunity of Electric Automated Mobility Services*. Rocky Mountain Institute.).

186 Seba, T. 2014. *Clean Disruption of Energy and Transportation: How Silicon Valley Will Make Oil, Nuclear, Natural Gas, Coal, Electric Utilities and Conventional Cars Obsolete by 2030*. Clean Planet Ventures, California.

187 Wikipedia. Swanson's law. Accessed April 10.

188 Mahapatra, S. 2016. New low solar price record set in Chile — 2.91c per kWh! Clean Technica, August 18.

189 Kurzweil. 2001. The Law of Accelerating Returns. March 21.

190 McAlone, N. 2015. This man invented the digital camera in 1975 — and his bosses at Kodak never let it see the light

of day. Business Insider, August 17.

191 The Economist, 2012. The last Kokak moment? Jan 14.

192 Seba, T. 2014. *Clean Disruption of Energy and Transportation: How Silicon Valley Will Make Oil, Nuclear, Natural Gas, Coal, Electric Utilities and Conventional Cars Obsolete by 2030.* Clean Planet Ventures, California.

193 Wikipedia. Disruptive innovation. Accessed April 10, 2017.

194 AAPL Investors. 2017. iPhone US Pricing History.

195 Virki, T. 2007. Nokia's cheap phone tops electronics chart. Reuters, May 3.

196 Seba, T. 2014. *Clean Disruption of Energy and Transportation: How Silicon Valley Will Make Oil, Nuclear, Natural Gas, Coal, Electric Utilities and Conventional Cars Obsolete by 2030.* Clean Planet Ventures, California.

197 Downes, L., and Nunes, P. 2013. Big-Bang Disruption. March, Harvard Business Review.

198 Shafer, M., Smith, H., and Linder, J. 2005. The Power of Business Models. February. Business Horizons 48(3):199-207.

199 Sisario, B., and Russel, K. 2016. In Shift to Streaming, Music Business Has Lost Billions. The New York Times, March 24.

200 McHaney, S. 2015. In the age of streaming music, just how much is a listen worth? NPR, February 4.

201 Consumer Technology Association. 2016. IoT is getting much smarter. i3, March 21.

202 Wikipedia, Internet protocol suite. Accessed April 10, 2017.

203 IBM. Understand the fundamentals of IBM Blockchain. Accessed April 10, 2017.

204 ROS. About ROS. Accessed April 10, 2017.

205 Udacity. 2017. Free Course: Artificial Intelligence for Robotics by Georgia Tech.

206 Udacity. 2017. Self-Driving Car Challenge.

207 OSVehicle. EDIT: a new modular self-driving car, in white-label. Accessed on April 10.

208 Wikipedia. Economies of scale. Accessed on April 10.

209 Oremus, W. 2016. Tech Companies Are

Dominating the Stock Market as Never Before. Slate, July 29.

210 Fiegerman, S. 2012. The Experts Speak: Here's what people predicted when the iPhone came out. Business Insider, June 29.

211 Lunden, I. 2015. 6.1B Smartphone Users Globally by 2020, Overtaking Basic Fixed Phone Subscriptions. Tech Crunch, June 2.

212 Ibid.

213 InfoPlease. 2017. Total Population of the World by Decade, 1950 – 2050.

214 Kamath, M. 2015. To reach 50 million users Telephone took 75 years, Internet took 4 years however Angry Birds took only 35 days!! TechWorm, March 13.

Made in the USA
Middletown, DE
06 May 2021